A Season of Slaughter

THE BATTLE OF SPOTSYLVANIA COURT HOUSE, MAY 8-21, 1864

By Chris Mackowski
and Kristopher D. White

EMERGING CIVIL WAR SERIES

Also part of the Emerging Civil War Series:

Simply Murder: The Battle of Fredericksburg, December 13, 1862
    by Chris Mackowski and Kristopher D. White

*The Last Days of Stonewall Jackson: The Mortal Wounding
of the Confederacy's Greatest Icon*
    by Chris Mackowski and Kristopher D. White

Also by Chris Mackowski and Kristopher D. White

*Chancellorsville's Forgotten Front: The Battles of Second Fredericksburg and
    Salem Church, May 3, 1863*

Also by Chris Mackowski

*The Dark, Close Wood: The Wilderness, Ellwood, and
    the Battle that Redefined Both*

Chancellorsville: Crossroads of Fire

A Season of Slaughter

THE BATTLE OF SPOTSYLVANIA
COURT HOUSE, MAY 8-21, 1864

By Chris Mackowski
and Kristopher D. White

EMERGING CIVIL WAR SERIES

SB
Savas Beatie
California

First edition, first printing 2013

ISBN-13: 978-1-61121-148-1

Library of Congress Cataloging-in-Publication Data

Mackowski, Chris.
Season of slaughter : the battle of Spotsylvania Court House, may 8-21, 1864 / by Chris Mackowski and Kristopher D. White. -- First Savas Beatie edition.
    pages cm
    ISBN 978-1-61121-148-1
    1. Spotsylvania Court House, Battle of, Va., 1864. I. White, Kristopher D. II. Title.
    E476.52.M34 2013
    973.7'36--dc23
    2013010923

SB

Published by
Savas Beatie LLC
989 Governor Drive, Suite 102
El Dorado Hills, California 95762
Phone: 916-941-6896
Email: sales@savasbeatie.com
Web: www.savasbeatie.com

Savas Beatie titles are available at special discounts for bulk purchases in the United States by corporations, institutions, and other organizations. For more details, please contact Special Sales, P.O. Box 4527, El Dorado Hills, CA 95762, or you may e-mail us as at sales@savasbeatie.com, or visit our website at www.savasbeatie.com for additional information.

KRIS: For Colton and Trevor

CHRIS: For Caity Stuart

We jointly dedicate this book to Greg Mertz, who taught us that good interpretation is like a puff of fresh air. This balloon is for you.

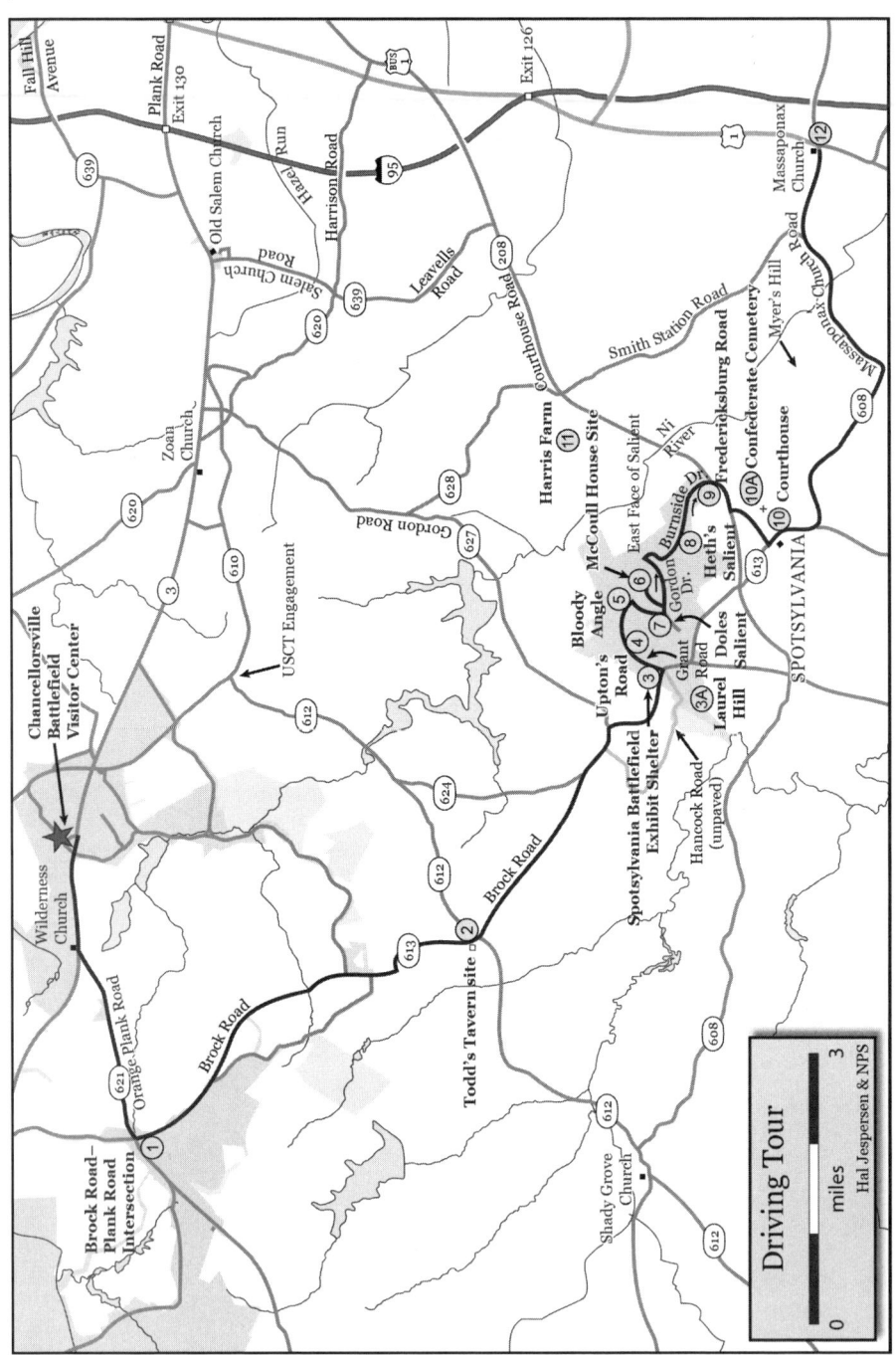

Driving Tour

0 — miles — 3

Hal Jespersen & NPS

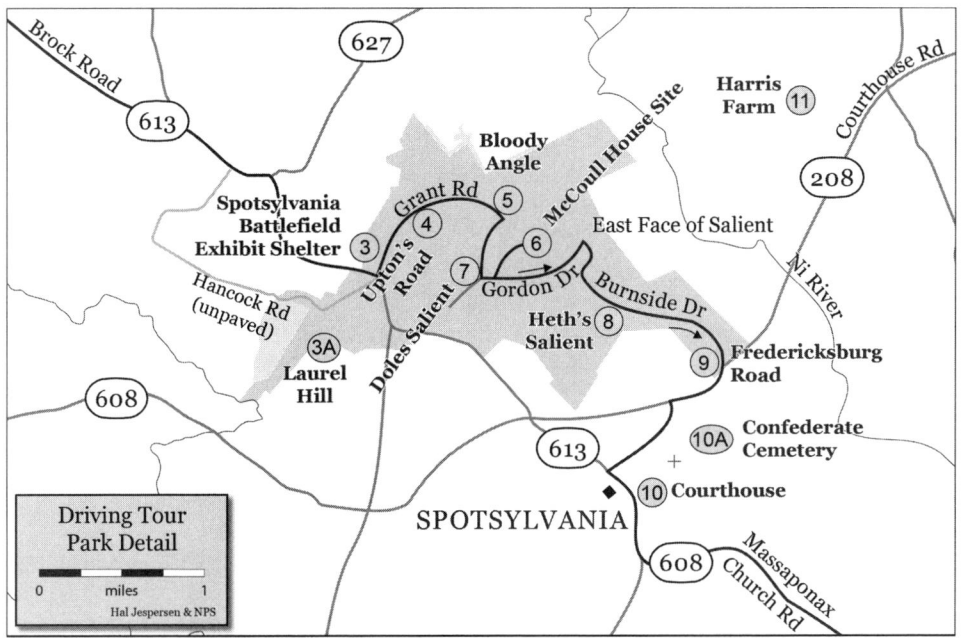

Touring the Battlefield

To give you a comprehensive look at the battlefield, this book deviates from the traditional Park Service driving tour. Directions at the end of each chapter will help you follow along. At times, this tour follows the course laid out by the Park Service; at other times, it goes completely out of the park and off park lands. Important preservation work by cooperating organizations such as the Civil War Trust and the Central Virginia Battlefields Trust have saved many of these properties and made them available to future generations. Please lend your support to their work. In some instances, this tour will refer to privately owned properties. Please do not trespass.

Keep in mind that some roads are one-way, and others may have heavy traffic. At times, you will be driving through neighborhoods and towns. Please follow all speed limits and park only in designated parking areas.

List of Maps

Maps by Hal Jespersen

Table of Contents

Acknowledgments

For years, the two of us worked together at the Stonewall Jackson Shrine on May 10, the anniversary of Jackson's death. It's also the anniversary, one year later, of Emory Upton's attack on Doles' Salient at Spotsylvania. Our good friend and Emerging Civil War author Daniel Davis is a big Upton fan, so after closing the Shrine, we'd meet with Dan out at Spotsy and, smoking cigars, we'd step off at 6:30 p.m. to retrace the steps of Upton's men in real time. That's how we fell in love with Spotsy.

At Fredericksburg and Spotsylvania National Military Park (FSNMP), we thank our friends Greg Mertz, Frank O'Reilly, Donald Pfanz, Tom Breen, Noel Harrison, Steward Henderson, Kathleen Logothetis, Ryan Longfellow, Eric Mink, and Beth Parnicza. Don's excellent monument study, *History Through Eyes of Stone*, served as an invaluable resource for this book, as did Noel's *Spotsylvania Gazetteer*. Local historian John Cummings has also been a wealth of information over the years. We thank, too, John Hennessy, chief of interpretation at FSNMP.

Dave Roth of *Blue and Gray* magazine gave us our first chance to write about Spotsy. For the Vol. 26 #1 issue in 2009, we wrote a detailed battle study of the action at the Mule Shoe; for the Vol. 27 #6 issue in 2011, we wrote about the oft-overlooked action between May 13-21. The issues completed a series started by our friend Greg Mertz, who wrote issues about Laurel Hill/Spindle Field and Upton's Attack. Readers who'd like to flesh out the story of Spotsylvania after they've finished this book will find those issues to be a great next step.

At the Russell J. Jandoli School of Journalism and Mass Communication at St. Bonaventure University, thanks go to Dean Pauline Hoffmann, Patrick "Mr. Bad Example" Vecchio, and Suzzane Ciesla and her fantastic staff of work-study students who handle so many of the little odds and ends for us as we keep our research organized.

At Savas Beatie, we thank first of all the remarkable and ever-energetic Theodore P. Savas, whose belief in our work continues to fuel us to do great things. Sarah Keeney deserves our thanks, too, for so ably managing the multitude of daily tasks required to keep us all on track. Thanks to Lindy Gervin, Veronica Kane, Yvette Lewis, and the entire staff for all their behind-the-scenes support.

Finally, thanks to all the authors at Emerging Civil War—a great bunch of friends and authors.

KRIS: To my wife Sarah, who endures many a night and weekend without a husband as I work on project after project.

To my parents, Donna and Evan, who were the first to take me to the Wilderness and Spotsylvania during the summer of 1994. Time and again they allowed me to drag them through the woods and fields of Virginia during the hottest time of year. They are the reason I am who I am today.

To my sisters, brothers, and nephews who have supported all my efforts, and have seen me grow as a student of history through the years.

To my co-author and best friend, Chris Mackowski, for his tireless efforts in getting this manuscript perfected and to press.

CHRIS: My daughter Stephanie—with whom I've shared so many of my best Civil War adventures—first introduced me to the Bloody Angle. She was four, and she liked the name. My thanks go out to her for the many wonderful walks we've shared out there in the years since.

My thanks go, too, to her brother, Jackson. Jackson patiently sat with me many nights running as I worked on this manuscript. His patience and forbearance have allowed you to hold this book in your hands.

No one is as present for me at Spotsy than Caity Stuart, with whom I shared many rich experiences on the battlefield. She will ever be everywhere there.

Thanks, as well, to Heidi Hartley, Claire Highwater, Sarah White, and, of course, Kris White. Time for another cigar, my friend.

Photo Credits:

Historical photos courtesy of Fredericksburg and Spotsylvania National Military Park except: Mott (pg. 64) courtesy the Library of Congress; Rosser (pg. 117) courtesy the Museum of the Confederacy; Ferrero (pg. 18) courtesy the Library of Congress; Burke (pg. 118) courtesy Steward Henderson; O'Sullivan (pg. 137) courtesy the Library of Congress; Sheridan and staff (pg. 144) courtesy Daniel T. Davis.

Modern photography by Chris Mackowski except: Harrison house site pictures (pp. 160-163) by Caity Stuart; Stuart monument (pg. 163) by Donald Pfanz.

xi

One thing is certain
of this campaign thus far,
and that is that more blood
has been shed, more lives lost,
and more human suffering undergone,
than ever before in a season.

— *Dr. Daniel Holt*
  121st New York Infantry

Prologue

The steel-gray morning of May 13, 1864, dawned with a light drizzle and a soundtrack of agony. For nearly 24 hours, the Army of the Potomac and the Army of Northern Virginia had savaged each other in hand-to-hand combat just outside Spotsylvania Court House. The Federal army had struck with size and power; the Confederate army, staving off near disaster, countered with desperation. The heavens downpoured on them.

In the wake of that fight, Confederates retreated to a stronger position, leaving Federals in possession of a battlefield so horrific that one officer described it as "a perfect Golgotha."

"In this angle of death the dead and wounded rebels lie, literally in piles—men in the agonies of death groaning beneath the dead bodies of their comrades," he wrote. Another called it "a terrible sight that would make one's blood run cold."

From the treeline where the Federal advance had emerged from the forest, across an open field of the Landrum farm, down into a swale and then back up again to the lip of the Confederate works, blue bodies carpeted the landscape. "In many places the dead and wounded lay three and four deep, with muskets, cartridge boxes, blankets, and everything pertaining to a soldier's gear, all in the wildest confusion," a member of the 110th Ohio later wrote:

One of the thousands of dead at Spotsylvania (inset)

A full moon rises over the Bloody Angle at the Spotsylvania Court House battlefield.

> *The face and parallel ditches were filled with water and blood, and the dead, from the rains, were bleached and ghastly. In many cases the wounded were so tangled and wedged in among the dead as to be utterly unable to extricate themselves without our help. God grant that such another slaughter may never occur.*

**"O God, what a fearful sight,"
one stretcher bearer wrote.**

"For fully a quarter of a mile I could have walked upon the slain, stepping from body to body on our side of the works," a New York officer said.

At the works themselves, the bodies were stacked upon each other in heaps, making "a perfect rampart of dead… on either side."

"Capt Lamont…fell just on the brow of this crest, early in the action," wrote Isaac Best of the 121st New York. "He was a finely developed man of perhaps 200 pounds weight, but his body was simply a mass of riddled flesh. I do not think that a square inch of surface was left without a bullet hole in it. From 9:30 a.m. to 5:30 p.m. he had been in the path of the bullets of both sides and fully exposed to them."

Soldiers in the 26th Michigan described the similar fate of one of their mates. "[H]ad it not been for some of his comrades who had seen him fall and identified the place, we would never have recognized it as having been a soldier," one later wrote. "There was no semblance of humanity about the mass that was lying before us. The only thing I could liken it to was a sponge, I presume five thousand bullets had passed through it; and after a careful search the largest piece we could find was three links of [his watch] chain, not to exceed one-quarter of an inch in length; the watch was entirely shot away."

Inside the abandoned works, the scene was just as grisly. "The lips of the dead were incrusted with powder from biting cartridges," said one Federal. "It was a horrible scene."

"The cellars were crowded with dead and wounded,

In the years after the battle, a sign nailed to a tree at the Bloody Angle called out the bivouac of the dead.

lying in some cases upon each other and in several inches of mud and water," a Wisconsinite wrote. "I saw the body of a rebel soldier sitting in the corner of one of these cellars in a position of apparent ease, with the head entirely gone, and the flesh burned from the bones and neck and shoulders." A Confederate lieutenant lay a short distance away with "twenty-one bullet holes in his body and an iron ramrod through his neck," another soldier reported.

Bodies were so mangled that burying parties, when they finally set to work later that morning, were obliged to scoop remains into blankets before they could be taken to the grave. "O God, what a sight, fearful to pen in my book…" wrote Maurus Oestreich, a stretcher-bearer from the 96th Pennsylvania. "I have seen so much that I can't nor will put it in this book. I will seal this in my memory by myself."

The swale in front of the Bloody Angle funneled Union soldiers straight into the melee.

"God have mercy on those who started this cruel war."

⟶ TO STOP 1

From the Chancellorsville Visitor Center parking lot, drive to the intersection of the parking lot and Bullock Road and turn left at the yield sign. At the stop sign at Route 3 (Orange Plank Road), turn right and travel 1.2 miles to the intersection of Route 3 and Route 621. At the light, turn left and follow Route 621 2.1 miles to the intersection of routes 621 and 613. At the stop sign, go straight for 275 feet and turn left into the parking area for the Brock Road/ Plank Road intersection.

GPS: N 38° .30078 W 77° .70940

The Campaign
CHAPTER ONE
MAY 1864

"It has been nothing but one scene of horror and blood shed since we crossed the Rapidan," wrote Pvt. Ransom F. Sargent in a letter. It was May 19, 1864—the first day in nearly three weeks that the musician from the 11th New Hampshire had the chance to sit down and write a letter. Sargent and his regiment—like the rest of the Army of the Potomac—had been relentlessly marching, fighting, and maneuvering through oppressive heat, pouring rain, pitch-black night, impenetrable wilderness, and apocalyptic forest fires—all in hostile territory.

The movement started on May 3, 1864, when Lt. Gen. Ulysses S. Grant, commanding all Union armies, ordered the Army of the Potomac to march south from its winter quarters around Culpepper and Brandy Station Virginia. The army's mission: "to hammer continuously against the armed force of the enemy and his resources, until by mere attrition, if in no other way, there should be nothing left to him." This represented a significant shift in strategy. Previous Union efforts had been aimed at the Confederate capital, not the Confederate armies: "On to Richmond!" Northerners cried.

Grant had other ideas. "Lee's army will be your objective," he told Maj. Gen. George Gordon Meade, commander of the Army of the Potomac. "Wherever Lee goes, there you will go also." Grant knew that if the vaunted defenders of Richmond were vanquished, nothing would stop the Union juggernaut from then just marching through the capital's front door.

Grant intended Meade's army to move in concert with several other Union armies: Maj. Gen. Benjamin Butler's

Lt. Gen. Ulysses S. Grant (inset)

The Brock Road/Plank Road intersection today

Army of the Potomac commander Maj. Gen. George G. Meade (left)

Army of Northern Virginia commander Gen. Robert E. Lee (right)

Army of the James was to move up the Virginia Peninsula and threaten Richmond from the southeast while Maj. Gen. Franz Sigel moved southward up the Shenandoah Valley, securing the breadbasket of the Confederacy; Maj. Gen. William Tecumseh Sherman's army group, consisting of the Armies of the Tennessee, Ohio, and Cumberland, were to push into Georgia toward Atlanta; and Maj. Gen. Nathaniel P. Banks' Army of the Gulf was to push from New Orleans toward Mobile, Alabama. The coordinated effort would prevent Confederates from using their interior lines to shift reinforcements from one theater of battle to another, "preventing him from using the same force at different sections against first one and then another of our armies," Grant wrote.

Under this strategy, Grant intended to apply pressure on all points of the Confederacy while letting each army commander call his own shots, even as he kept a big-picture eye on everything. However, he felt the Army of the Potomac deserved special attention because of its high-profile position so close to the capital and the population and media centers of the east—not to mention the difficulties that army traditionally had with its Confederate counterpart, the Army of Northern Virginia. As a result, Grant chose to make his headquarters in the field with Meade's army, although he still intended to let Meade execute the actual day-to-day operation of the army. Grant would also shield Meade from the politics of Washington.

Meade, so irascible that his men called him a "godammed google-eyed snapping turtle," had actually expected Grant to sack him in favor of a hand-picked successor, and so Meade had even offered Grant his resignation. The gesture so impressed Grant that he kept Meade in command of the army.

"[Grant] is so much more active than his predecessor, and agrees so well with me in his views, I cannot but be rejoiced at his arrival, because I believe my success to be the more probable," Meade wrote in a letter to his wife. "My duty is plain, to continue quietly to discharge my duties, heartily co-operating with him and under him."

Under Grant's orders, Meade moved the Army of

Grant spent so much time in the field among his men that he earned a reputation for being rumpled and dusty. An observer once described him as "the dust-covered man."

the Potomac southward on May 3 with an eye toward the open country around Spotsylvania Court House. There, the army would have several possible avenues of approach toward Richmond. Although the Confederate capital was not the army's true objective, the Federal commanders reasoned that, by threatening the city, they could draw the Army of Northern Virginia out into the open for a decisive battle. With just over 123,000 men, the Federal army would hold a significant numerical advantage in any such contest.

First, the Federal army had to move through an area known as the Wilderness—70 square miles of nearly impenetrable second-growth forest. "[A] most appropriate term," said Theodore Lyman, a member of Meade's staff, "a land of an exhausted, sandy soil, supporting more or less dense growth of pine or of oak. There are some cleared spaces, especially near the Germanna plank . . . The very worst of it is parallel with the Orange Plank and upper part of the Brock Road."

"This Wilderness is a generally level barren, covered with a matted growth of scrub oak, stunted pine, sweet gum brush and dogwood," recounted Col. S. D. Thurston of the 3rd North Carolina. "The surface of the earth is indented occasionally with low basins, through which the rainfall, washing from the higher margins, cuts long gullies and often deep and wide washouts."

It was here in the Wilderness, on the morning of May 5, where things started to go wrong for Ulysses S. Grant.

*   *   *

After an autumn of cat-and-mouse with the Army of the Potomac, the Army of Northern Virginia had settled

"LEE'S ARMY WILL BE YOUR OBJECTIVE. WHEREVER LEE GOES, THERE YOU WILL GO ALSO."

The Second Corps fortified its position along the Brock Road in the Wilderness.

into winter camps along a defensive line that paralleled the Rapidan River, from an area along the edge of the Wilderness westward toward Orange Court House. The army's First Corps, under Lt. Gen. James Longstreet, had been away on detached service in Tennessee for much of that time but returned in April, bringing Confederate strength up to 66,000 men fit for duty. Although Lee didn't know the exact strength of his Federal counterparts, he knew they outnumbered him significantly.

Ever audacious, Lee looked for a way to even the odds through mobility and surprise. When he got word about the Federal movement, he first assumed the Army of the Potomac would turn westward and strike him directly—but as soon as he realized the Federals were marching southeast, he decided to take the fight to them. Striking out along parallel roads, Lee launched the Army of Northern Virginia into the exposed flank of the Federal column as it tried to march through the Wilderness.

Initially, Grant planned to move through the area in a single day, but much to his chagrin, the Army of the Potomac plodded along at a far slower pace than anticipated. During his time in the Western Theater, Grant had commanded fast-marching, hard-scrabble armies that adapted on the fly and responded quickly to his orders. The much larger Army of the Potomac, however, proved to be a far more ungainly creature. As May 4 wore on, it became apparent that the army would not clear the Wilderness. Meade ordered the army to camp for the night and resume the march toward Spotsylvania in the morning.

But when morning arrived, so did Lee's army, and the sight of Confederates proved too tempting for Grant to resist. "If any opportunity presents itself of pitching into a part of Lee's Army," Grant said, "do so without giving time for disposition." Fifth Corps commander Maj. Gen. Gouverneur K. Warren—leading the corps into battle for the first time, and therefore eager to prove himself a capable fighter—deployed his men for attack. The resulting engagement in Saunders field opened a two-day slugfest that proved to be one of the bloodiest battles of the war.

The Wilderness worked against Federals because Meade couldn't bring the full weight of his army online. The Wilderness offered no room for maneuver, thereby countering any advantage his numbers might otherwise have given him. Similarly, cavalry had very little room to maneuver, and artillery had few places to deploy.

As shrewdly as Lee used the terrain to equalize the odds, he failed to gain a fuller advantage because he could only feed his army into the fight piecemeal. Poor communication among his subordinates led to poor coordination, which in turn led to several Federal breakthroughs—averted each time by Confederate audacity and luck. That luck finally ran out on May 6 when Longstreet, appearing on the scene at quite literally the nick of time, was accidentally shot by his own men while executing a surprise flank attack. Longstreet's wounding, while not fatal, would knock him out of the campaign—an incident that would have serious implications for Lee in the days to follow.

The see-saw fighting on May 6 ground into a stalemate that Grant knew he could not break. On the morning of May 7, he cut orders to begin a withdrawal from the Wilderness. Once more, thought the soldiers of the Army of the Potomac, they had run into Bobby Lee and come up short, and once more, their new commander was going to pack it in and turn tail.

That all changed on the evening of May 7. With the Wilderness burning around them, Grant and Meade and their staffs rode down to the scene of the battle's worst fighting, the intersection of the Brock Road and Plank Road. It was the most important crossroad of Grant's life. He could direct the army eastward along the Plank Road, out of the Wilderness and back toward the safety of the Rappahannock River or Fredericksburg. Every other defeated Union commander had executed a similar retreat following a drubbing from Lee, and everyone expected Grant to do the same.

Instead, Grant ordered the army southeast along the Brock Road toward the crossroads town of Spotsylvania Court House.

The morale of the men soared as they realized the army was moving toward the enemy, not away from it as the army had done so many times before. "[The army] has obtained a grip upon the throat of the Confederacy," one officer said, "a grip that will not be relaxed until treason gasps and dies."

If he could not outfight Lee in the Wilderness, Grant intended to outflank him.

At the Brock Road / Plank Road Intersection

Standing at the Brock Road/Plank Road intersection today, it's hard to imagine: the entire war turned at this point. Had Grant chosen to retreat from the Wilderness, Confederates would have had one more notch to add to their string of victories, and Gettysburg, ten months earlier, would have been remembered in history as the same kind of setback Antietam had been. Otherwise, how could Gettysburg have been "the" turning point if Confederates bounced back with another win? By moving around Lee's left and moving south, Grant refused to be beaten.

Today, the Wilderness is hardly wild. With several major subdivisions tucked away beyond the forest that lines the road, thousands of people make their homes there. What had once been a quiet intersection in the dark, close wood is now one of the busiest places on any of the area battlefields. Watch for traffic if you get out to look around.

Off the parking area on the southwest corner of the intersection, a half-mile footpath winds through the forest, covering ground where fighting took place on May 6. The forest today is much more mature than it was in 1864, so the trees now stand taller, with more open space in the understory. In 1864, though, this second-growth forest was nearly impenetrable to see through let alone move through.

The Wilderness has been remembered, in particular, for its own special brand of Hell: in more than a dozen places, the tinder-dry leaves from the previous autumn caught fire. "Swept by the flames, the trees, bushes, and logs which the Confederates had thrown up as breastworks . . . took fire and dense clouds of smoke rolled across the clearing, choking the unfortunates who were exposed to it, and greatly hindering the work of the rescuers," the

Soldiers cheered Grant wildly when they realized he was leading them onward, not rearward.

historian of the 146th New York recalled. "The clearing now became a raging inferno, in which many of the wounded perished and the bodies of the dead were blackened and burned beyond all possibility of recognition, a tragic conclusion to this day of horror."

Along the hiking path, visitors will pass numerous interpretive markers, as well as the monument to the Vermont Brigade, placed on the battlefield in 2006. A pair of monuments to the 12th New Jersey Volunteers sits next to the roadside.

The remains of three lines of Federal earthworks also run through the area, although the Orange Plank Road bisects through them. The earthworks formed a defense in depth for the Federals, who needed all three lines to resist a Confederate breakthrough.

The earthworks caught fire during those charges. Through the night and the next day, much of the forest in this area burned, too. Picture Grant and Meade and their staffs riding into that inferno, their exhausted troops expecting retreat, only to have the general in chief lead them south. "Soldiers weary and sleepy after their long battle, with stiffened limbs and smarting wounds, now sprang to their feet forget of their pains, and rushed forward to the roadside," one of Grant's staffers later wrote. "Wild cheers echoed through the forest, and glad shouts of triumph rent the air. Men swung their hats, tossed up their arms, and pressed forward to within touch of their chief, clapping their hands, and speaking to him with the familiarity of comrades."

Sketch of the Army of the Potomac moving south

Also of note just down the Orange Plank Road three-tenths of a mile is the spot where Confederate Lt. Gen. James Longstreet was accidentally shot by his own men on May 6, 1864—an event that would have serious repercussions for the campaign ahead. The incident robbed Lee of his "Old Warhorse" at a time when he would need him most, under circumstances that would play to Longstreet's greatest strength. Although the First Corps commander could hit like a hammer on the offense, he had a particular skill at defensive warfare. The battles at Spotsylvania would have been just his style.

The First Corps, hunkered down in this area, began its march toward Spotsylvania from here (see next chapter). Most of the road cut for them by Brig. Gen. William Pendleton no longer exists, obliterated by a housing development. The mouth of the road, while still there, sits on private property not accessible to visitors. The other roads Anderson used to get to the battlefield still exist, however, (see map on pg. 16) and they can lead visitors on a circuitous route to the Spotsylvania battlefield.

Out of the Wilderness

CHAPTER TWO

MAY 7, 1864

The similarities seem almost eerie. On May 2, 1863, Second Corps commander Lt. Gen. Thomas Jonathan "Stonewall" Jackson's own men accidentally shot him as they successfully executed a surprise flank attack through the Wilderness at the battle of Chancellorsville. One year and four days later on May 6, 1864, less than five miles away, First Corps commander Lt. Gen. James Longstreet's own men accidentally shot him as they successfully executed a surprise flank attack through the Wilderness.

Without Longstreet, whom Lee called his "Old Warhorse," the Southern army faced the most serious leadership crisis of the war. Longstreet was Lee's most experienced and most trusted lieutenant, and he depended heavily on him. Lee's other two senior generals—Ewell and Hill—meanwhile, had underperformed in the year since their elevation to corps command. Longstreet's absence left Lee without a steady shoulder to lean on.

Fortunately for Lee, the morning of May 7 brought only sporadic skirmishing between his forces and the Army of the Potomac. He had brought the Federals to heel and, for two days, bloodied them savagely. While Lee had not gained any tactical advantage, the Army of Northern Virginia still maintained a relatively strong defensive position. Lee needed only wait out Grant's next move. In the meantime, he turned his attention to the pressing question of leadership for the First Corps.

No one seemed perfect. One option: Maj. Gen.

Maj. Gen. Richard Anderson (inset)

"[C]oming out of the Wilderness, is about the same as coming out of a dark house or room into the open air where the sun is shining," one Confederate said.

9

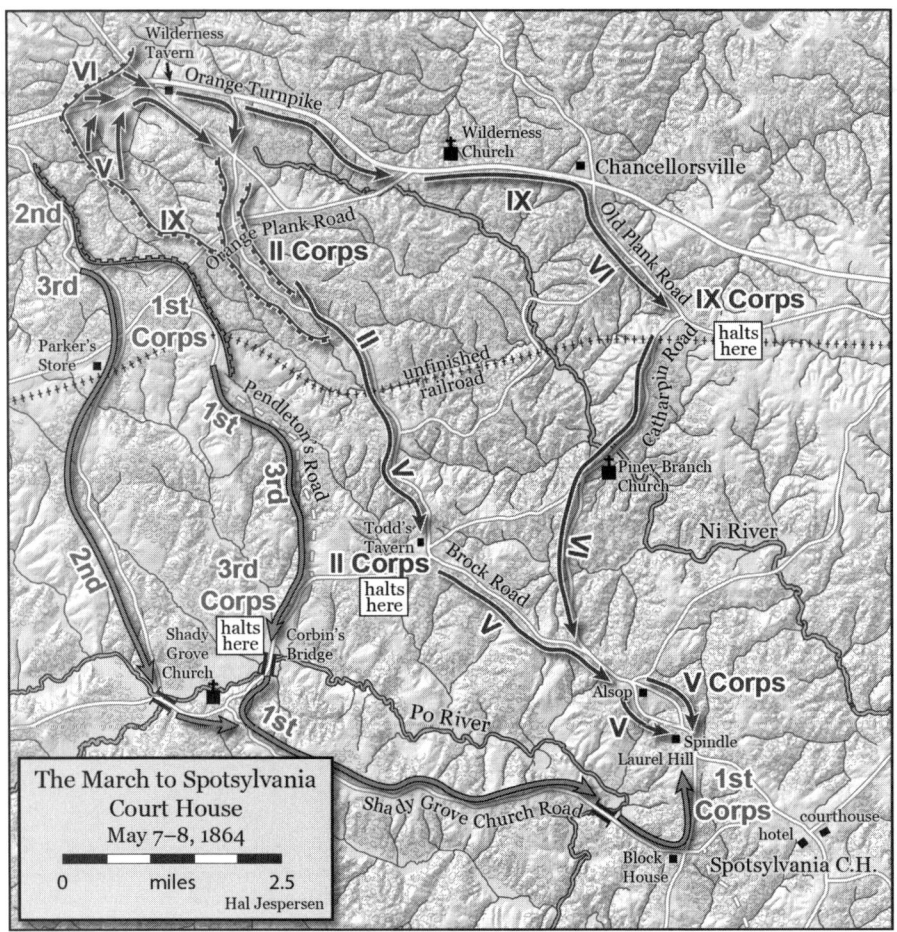

The March to Spotsylvania
Court House
May 7–8, 1864

0   miles   2.5

Hal Jespersen

**THE MARCH TO
SPOTSYLVANIA COURT HOUSE**
Confederates carved their own
road out of the Wilderness,
then took a roundabout march
to beat Federals to Spotsylvania
Court House. Federals, stymied
by Confederate cavalry, were
further hampered by the size
of their own army as it tried to
move over clogged roads.

Edward "Allegheny" Johnson, a hard-fighting division
commander from the Second Corps who'd served with
distinction since his early days under Stonewall Jackson
during the '62 Valley campaign—but as a Second Corps
commander, he was, in one staff officer's words, "quite
unknown" to the First Corps.

A second option: Maj. Gen. Jubal Early, "Old Jube"
as his men called him. Lee called him "my bad old man."
Irascible and profane, Early had proven himself time and
again a go-to division commander in the Second Corps,
serving with particular distinction at both First and Second
Fredericksburg, but his abrasive personality had earned
him enemies in the First Corps.

Lee nonetheless seemed to lean in Early's direction—
thus surprising everyone later that morning when he
promoted a dark horse candidate, Maj. Gen. Richard H.
Anderson, commander of the First Corps' third division.
The 42-year-old Anderson, while not a spectacular choice,

was certainly a safe one—"as pleasant a commander to serve under as could be wished, and was a sturdy and reliable fighter," one Confederate said.

A graduate of West Point's class of 1842, Anderson had been promoted for gallantry during the Mexican War. His postwar army career included stints as a recruiter, time on the Texas frontier, service in Kansas during border troubles in 1856-57, and service in the Mormon War of 1858-59. When his native South Carolina seceded, Anderson resigned his commission and went with the South. He steadily rose through the Confederate army, with notable service on the Peninsula in 1862 and at Chancellorsville in 1863. After Lee reshuffled the army into three corps, Anderson served under Maj. Gen. A. P. Hill in the Third Corps, but the men of the First still knew him well.

Anderson had little time to settle into his new command. Lee, trying to anticipate Grant's next move as the day wore on, set Anderson into motion almost at once. "I have reasons to believe that the enemy is withdrawing his forces from our front and will strike us next at [Spotsylvania]," Lee told him. "I wish you to be there to meet him."

Spotsylvania Court House, Lee knew, provided a road network that would open a variety of options for the Federal army should Grant move there: multiple approaches to Richmond and shorter supply routes and more secure communication lines from Washington. The First Corps served as Lee's right flank and so was in the best position to move southward to block any such Federal movement.

The Confederates had no road to move by, though. Despite repeated attempts by Lee to dislodge them on May 6, Grant's men controlled the Brock Road/Plank Road intersection. The Brock Road—the main road south out of the Wilderness—gave Grant a direct, unimpeded route to Spotsylvania; Lee had dense forest blocking his way.

In anticipation of the move, Lee ordered his chief of artillery, Brig. Gen. William Pendleton, to oversee construction of a new road. Lee's men would, in effect, cut their own way out of the Wilderness.

Lee instructed Anderson to move "[a]s soon after dark as you can effect it," keeping the withdrawal a secret from Federals. "[M]arch the troops a little way to the rear and let them have some sleep," Lee ordered.

Ironically, Lee "forbid fire or any noise that might give intelligence of the withdrawal." To Anderson's chagrin, he "found the woods on fire and burning furiously in every direction, and there was no suitable place for a rest." To escape the flames, Anderson started his men south some four hours earlier than anticipated—a decision that would

Lt. Gen. James Longstreet survived the horrid wound to his right shoulder and throat he received in the Wilderness but did not return to Lee's army until October 1864. By then, the army was being strangled in the siege around Petersburg. Of Lee's most famous lieutenants, Stuart Jackson, and Longstreet himself, Old Pete was the only one to survive the war, but in the postwar years earned a reputation as a "scalawag" to many Confederate veterans because he became both a Catholic and Republican, and he supported Ulysses S. Grant's presidential campaign. As a reward, Grant appointed him surveyor of customs in New Orleans; later, President Rutherford B. Hayes appointed him U.S. Minister to Turkey. Longstreet also served as a U.S. commissioner of railroads in the late 1890s. A headstrong man, Longstreet made the mistake of being an outspoken critic of the way Lee handled the army, earning him the eternal ire of Lost Cause revisionists ever since. Lee's former second-in-command died on January 2, 1904, six days before his 83rd birthday. He is buried in Alta Vista Cemetery in Gainseville, Georgia.

have important ramifications come morning.

The Third Corps, which held the center of the Confederate position, filled in the space left by the First Corps; in turn, the Second Corps, holding the Confederate left flank, shifted, as well. Lee ordered both corps to fall into line of march once it became clear Grant was actually moving south, too.

Confederates left behind such a scene of devastation as most had never seen. "The spectacle was most distressing," a South Carolinian in the Third Corps said:

> *From a thick wilderness of stunted saplings, unbroken by a hog path, the place had become a charred, torn, open woods, cut up with numerous narrow wagon roads. Every tree seemed to be riddled with balls. Small arms, mostly broken or bent, strewed the ground, with every conceivable damaged article of accoutrement or clothing, and graves, filled with the dead of both armies, were fearfully frequent. Horses lay unburied. The stench of burning vegetable matter and clothing, and the gases steaming up through the thin covering of the graves, almost suffocated me in the hot, close air of the forest.*

After two days of intense fighting and another of nerve-wracking skirmishing, the march out of the Wilderness was, according to some, "the hardest march of the war."

"It seemed like it was almost beyond human endurance," said an Alabamian in the Second Corps. "Our route lay through the wilderness, a country covered by dense undergrowth. It was a hot day along a narrow dusty road, and to add to the heat

On the march from the Wilderness

and thirst the woods on both sides of the road were on fire and suffocation almost was annoying us. Many began to faint from over exertion and the road was lined with exhausted men."

"There was very little water on the way," the South Carolinian added, "and the heat was most debilitating."

At least one Virginian tried to put a positive spin on the move. "At least we are out of the woods," he said, "and the difference between the two, coming out of the Wilderness, is about the same as coming out of a dark house or room into the open air where the sun is shining."

*   *   *

To manage the flow of troops, Lee sent Anderson down the newly cut "Pendleton Road," followed by A. P. Hill's Third Corps. The road, which ran roughly parallel to the Brock Road, intersected with the Catharpin Road between Corbin's Bridge to the southwest and Todd's Tavern to the east. Elements of Brig. Gen. Wade Hampton's cavalry brigade protected the approach from Todd's Tavern, allowing the First Corps column to move through unmolested.

The Second Corps, meanwhile, fell back along the Plank Road toward Parker's Store, and then cut southward through the Wilderness toward Shady Grove Church, situated along the Catharpin Road south of Corbin's Bridge. The two corps, Second and First, met at the intersection of Shady Grove Church Road, which branched southeast toward Spotsylvania Court House. Anderson's exhausted corps hustled through the intersection first.

"The road by which I was conducted was narrow and frequently obstructed; so that at best the progress of the troops was slow," Anderson later reported:

Confederate Lt. Gen. A. P. Hill, commander of the Confederate Third Corps, fell ill during the move out of the Wilderness. Maj. Gen. Jubal Early, a division commander from Second Corps, would serve as his temporary replacement.

> [T]he guide having informed me that it preserved the same character until near Spottsylvania Court-house, I found some open fields, and halted there to let the troops close up and rest a little. The orders to this effect had scarcely been given when a courier from Fitzhugh Lee arrived with an urgent call from him to any troops that might be met to come to his support with all speed for his cavalry was hard pressed and could not hold the place much longer.

In response to the cavalryman's summons, Anderson rallied his men back into motion.

"As we neared Spotsylvania," said one Confederate infantryman, "the rattling of musketry told us too plainly our day's trials were not over . . ."

➤ TO STOP 2

Turn right onto Route 621 (Orange Plank Road) and follow it 275 feet to the stop sign. At the stop sign, turn right onto Route 613 (Brock Road) and follow it for 4.7 miles. The parking area for Todd's Tavern will be on the right side of the road, opposite the site of the modern store.

GPS: N 38° .24749 W 77° .66877

Todd's Tavern
CHAPTER THREE
MAY 7-8, 1864

In the three years since the war began, Philip Sheridan's career had enjoyed a meteoric rise. In March of 1861, just before the outbreak of hostilities, he had been a freshly minted first lieutenant in the Regular Army, and by May, earned his captaincy. Within three years, he rocketed to major general and had earned a position as one of Grant's favorite subordinates. Sheridan was, Grant said, "the embodiment of heroism, dash, and impulse."

When Grant assumed command of all Union armies, he brought Sheridan east with him to command the Army of the Potomac's entire cavalry corps. "The officer you brought from the West is rather a little fellow to handle your cavalry," an officer at the War Department told Grant.

"You will find him big enough for the purpose before we get through with him," Grant replied.

President Lincoln described Sheridan as a "brown, chunky little chap, with a long body, short legs, not enough neck to hang him, and such arms that if his ankles itch he can scratch them without stooping." Standing 5'5" in his boots, Sheridan was a bandy-legged Irishman with a droopy moustache and boisterous personality. "Sheridan makes everywhere a favorable impression," one of George Meade's staff officers said.

Not that he made a favorable impression on Meade, though, who was his immediate supervisor. The two alpha males differed in their ideas on how to properly employ cavalry. Meade had used the cavalry as a picket screen for the army's winter camp, while Sheridan wanted to consolidate the cavalry and rest the men and horses, employing the infantry as pickets instead. In the end, Meade relented to

Maj. Gen. "Little Phil" Sherdian (inset)

Looking north along the Brock Road from the modern Todd's Tavern pull-off

15

his new subordinate's wishes, but tension remained.

Thus far in the spring campaign, Meade's concerns about Sheridan had bourn themselves out. On May 4 and 5, the cavalryman's troopers failed to properly locate the Army of Northern Virginia or report to army headquarters the Confederates' approach toward the Wilderness.

On May 6, Sheridan received word that the Federal left flank, held by Maj. Gen. Winfield S. Hancock's II Corps, had been turned. Meade ordered Sheridan to pull back the bulk of his cavalry to the Chancellorsville area to secure the Federal supply wagons. By May 7, however, it became evident that Hancock's left had not been turned. By then, Grant had made his decision to press on toward Richmond via the Brock Road. The job of opening the way and securing the army's vulnerable left flank fell to Sheridan's men.

A narrow farm lane barely wide enough for two wagons to pass each other, the Brock Road ran roughly north to south—10 miles from its intersection with the Orange Turnpike to its terminus with Courthouse Road. Along the way, a number of secondary roads intersected with it, sometimes intertwining with each other like snakes: the Furnace Road, the Catharpin Road, and the Piney Branch Church Road. On the morning of May 7, Sheridan instructed two of his three divisions to press west and south in an effort to clear the Brock Road of resistance.

Major General Fitzhugh Lee's Confederate cavalry division waited for them. On the evening of May 6, shortly after Sheridan's men pulled out of the area in response to the reported threat to Hancock, the Confederate troopers had arrived to take possession of the Brock Road/Catharpin Road intersection. There, they set up a defensive perimeter around Todd's Tavern by refacing earthworks that Sheridan's troopers had scratched out.

Brig. Gen. Wesley Merritt

Sheridan's plan to confront the awaiting Confederates was simple: He ordered his best division, under the command of Brig. Gen. Wesley Merritt, to move his 4,500 troopers west along the Furnace Road until they reached the Brock Road, then turn south toward Todd's Tavern. Meanwhile, Brig. Gen. David Gregg's division would push toward Todd's Tavern west along the Catharpin Road. If all went well, nearly 8,000 Union troopers would converge on Fitz Lee's front, right flank, and rear.

Merritt's column was led by the 24-year-old Brig. Gen. George A. Custer, perhaps the most famous Union cavalry officer who'd come out of the war. Custer's five Michigan regiments were among the best in the Federal service. They made it as far as the Furnace Road/Brock Road intersection without meeting any resistance, but once they turned south, the troopers made contact.

Brig. Gen. David Gregg

The 1st Michigan Cavalry pushed back, and the 6th New York Cavalry—the Second Ira Harris Guards—rode up in support. Their commander, Brig. Gen. Thomas Devin, was known as "Buford's Hard Hitter." His men

The Brock Road near
Todd's Tavern

extended the right end of the Union line, forcing the Rebels back toward the tavern lest they be flanked.

Even as he saw his line give ground to the north, Fitzhugh looked to the east and saw a dust cloud approaching along the Catharpin Road. Although his troopers had constructed a sturdy barricade at the intersection, Fitz realized his time at Todd's Tavern was up. He ordered a general withdrawal to the south, two miles closer to Spotsylvania Court House.

Around noon, Gregg's troopers thundered into the intersection. Merritt's men met up with them shortly thereafter. Although they had secured a key piece of real estate, they now had to expand the opening. Their next task was to push farther west along the Catharpin Road, which crossed the narrow Po River at a place called Corbin's Bridge. The Federal cavalry commanders knew they had to take the bridge, or at least maintain a defensive line near it, in order to protect the Federal army as it marched down the Brock Road. Otherwise, the Confederate army might slip across the bridge and attack the Army of the Potomac in the flank. So, Gregg secured the Catharpin Road/Brock Road intersection with two regiments, then pushed his other four regiments west.

The area, it turned out, remained flush with Confederate horsemen despite Fitz Lee's withdrawal. Major General Wade Hampton had arrived on the scene with his fresh division of troopers. Although not a West Point graduate, the South Carolina millionaire-turned-soldier had proven himself a highly capable commander nonetheless—and today, he stepped up again. With elements of two brigades, he pushed eastward until he struck resistance, near 3:00 p.m., less than a mile from Corbin's Bridge. Hampton's commander, Jeb Stuart, arrived on the scene, too, with elements of a third brigade.

Both sides fought dismounted. The Federals held a

Brig. Gen. Thomas Devin (center), "Buford's Heavy Hitter," surrounded by members of his staff

Brig. Gen. George Armstrong Custer

strong position, bolstered by hastily fashioned earthworks and a few pieces of artillery. As Confederates pushed into the open field against them, Federal fire threw them back. "[T]he rebel yell was turned into a whine as they quickly disappeared into the woods," a Union soldier said. Once protected by the trees, Confederates seemed content to exchange fire with the fortified Federals from a distance, not daring to again venture into the open.

Gregg's troopers, pleased with their gains, settled in for the night. They had secured the western side of Todd's Tavern.

* * *

Merritt's men, meanwhile, had pushed south from Todd's Tavern along the Brock Road toward Spotsylvania Court House. Leading the way were the as-yet-unengaged men of Merritt's third brigade, that of Col. Alfred Gibbs. Gibbs' men had arrived in the early afternoon after an unwelcome stint guarding the army's supply wagons. Custer's and Devin's brigades were given a much-needed rest as Gibbs' men rode to the front of the column.

They made it about one mile south of the tavern before Fitz Lee's men hit them with a volley. The Confederates had retreated, Federals discovered, but had not retreated far.

Again both sides fought dismounted. Gibbs kept feeding men into the fray until, at last, the Confederate skirmish line gave way. They fell back only far enough to link up with the main body of Fitz's men, though, nearly two miles south of Todd's Tavern, and there they made a determined stand. Fighting from behind barricades, Confederates held on while the Federals bloodied themselves against the works. "The head of our column was literally smashed in," one Federal said. When the works caught fire, the men battled one another through the flames—a scene that had

Dismounted cavalry blocked the roads to take advantage of cover.

become all too common during the campaign.

"For a half hour there was one of the hottest fights between opposing brigades of dismounted cavalry that occurred during the war," a Virginian recalled. But the Confederate line held.

Finally, near dusk, the Federal troopers pulled back toward Todd's Tavern. "The ground over which they charged was left blue with their slain," a Southerner observed.

The door to Spotsylvania Court House remained tightly shut.

* * *

Brig. Gen. Fitzhugh Lee

To the north, the first Federal infantry units began to withdraw from the main battle line in the Wilderness at around 8:00 p.m. Brigadier General John Robinson's V Corps division led the march through the dark, close woods, the glow of the burning forest sending eerie flickers of light through the trees to their rear. Along the roadside, the exhausted men of the II and VI corps tried to sleep; some stretched out in the road itself, and Robinson's men had to pick their way through.

Meade and Grant rode near the head of the column. As exhausted as he was, Meade and his staff at one point nearly rode into Confederate lines. Finally, near midnight, the column reached Todd's Tavern.

The sight that greeted Meade sent him skyrocketing. Sheridan's troopers, who were supposed to be in Spotsylvania Court House after clearing the road, had camped in and around Todd's Tavern—and cavalry commander Phil Sheridan was nowhere to be found.

The volatile Meade literally began kicking butts. He booted a number of sleeping troopers up and into their saddles, then immediately cut orders to both Gregg and Merritt to clear the road south. While the cavalry commanders scurried off, Meade's staff took over the tavern as a temporary headquarters. Outside, the footsore infantry halted. Many men sat where they stopped and tried to sleep.

Merritt's cavalry rode into the darkness to again engage with Fitz Lee's troopers—but again, they made little headway.

Brig. Gen. Wade Hampton

Infuriated and frustrated, Meade ordered Robinson's men to their feet and marched them to the front to do what the cavalry could not. "They had to be punched, kicked, and shaken up to learn that more fighting was in order, before either lodging or breakfast," an officer said.

With their rifled muskets, Robinson's infantry held the advantage of range over Fitz's cavalry. The cavalry, in turn, held the advantage of speed because of their horses. As Robinson's men closed the gap, the Confederates mounted up and pulled back to the next ridgeline, where they dismounted and again began to resist the Federal pursuit. "Numerous barricades were encountered, and trees were

The Union army marches past Todd's Tavern on the way to Spotsylvania Court House.

felled across the road," a staff officer recalled. Ridgeline to ridgeline, the Confederates stymied the Federals—but weren't able to actually stop them.

The deadly cat-and-mouse continued even as the sky lightened. Dawn came as did the Federals. "The opposition to us amounts to nothing as yet," Robinson wrote in a note to Meade a little while later.

By 8:00 a.m., Robinson's herky-jerky advance had pushed Fitz to within a mile of Spotsylvania Court House. There, Confederate cavalry commander Jeb Stuart arrived on the scene to orchestrate a last-ditch defense atop a low ridgeline named Laurel Hill. This was, Stuart knew, the last defensible position north of town. If the Confederate cavalry failed to hold, the Army of the Potomac would march straight into Spotsylvania and gain possession of the direct track to Richmond. The road network there would also give the Federals access to a new supply line. "Times were getting very serious with us," one cavalryman worried.

Even as Robinson massed his men for this latest push, Stuart saw reinforcements approach from his rear—"as if by magic," one soldier said. It was Richard Anderson's First Corps, answering Fitz Lee's urgent summons. Stuart immediately began to direct the infantrymen into line. "Hush, hush, boys," he told them, trying to maintain his newfound element of surprise. "Be quiet. Don't say a word." Stuart worked "cool as a piece of ice," one observer said, "though all the time laughing."

The race for Spotsylvania Court House was over; the battle of Spotsylvania Court House had now begun.

At Todd's Tavern

The original Todd's Tavern sat on the opposite side of the road from the current structure. Built by 1835, the tavern doubled as a store and post office, and several smaller outbuildings stood around it. It was, said a II Corps soldier, "an unpretentious structure one story and a half in height, with no merits, architectural or otherwise, to warrant its becoming a conspicuous landmark in the history of this campaign." A man named Flavius Bradshaw owned the tavern, but he rented it out to Charles Bradshaw, who operated it with his wife, Mary, with the help of one slave and a free black. The tavern survived the war but was destroyed in 1884.

A pull-off opposite the modern tavern offers a view of the fields to the west, now filled with electrical towers, where Wade Hampton's cavalry fended off David Gregg's cavalry, protecting Anderson's troops as they filed onto the Shady Grove Church Road from Pendleton's makeshift road through the woods. Gregg, ironically, thought he was fending off Confederates so the Federal army could file past Todd's Tavern.

The original Todd's Tavern (top) consisted of a small compound of buildings. It sat across the road from the site of the modern Todd's Tavern (bottom).

To the northeast, Catharpin Road heads off toward the Orange Plank Road. Where those two roads meet, Confederate cavalry under Thomas Rosser clashed with members of the United States Colored Troops on the afternoon of May 15—the first time black troops saw action against the Army of Northern Virginia. (See Chapter 13 for the complete story.)

Hancock worried the day away here on May 8, unable to get to the battlefield because the road ahead was so jammed with troops. His nerves on end, he let reports of Confederate movement to the west spook him. It was Hampton, still rattling around well enough to fool the Army of the Potomac's best corps commander. "And so the Second Corps stood to arms, all the afternoon and into the early evening," one of his men said, "believing that another of its great days of battle had come." But darkness set it, he added, "and the great battle of Todd's Tavern was never fought."

⟶ TO STOP 3 & 3A

From the Todd's Tavern site, turn right onto Route 613 (Brock Road) and follow it for 3.8 miles. The Spotsylvania Battlefield will be on the left even as Brock Road curves to the right. Turn left onto Grant Drive and follow it for 0.1 miles, then turn left into the Spotsylvania Exhibit Shelter.

GPS: N 38° .21908 W 77° .61420

Laurel Hill

CHAPTER FOUR

MAY 8, 1864

For the men of the Confederate First Corps, the previous few days had been little more than a high-stakes case of "Hurry Up."

Roused from their camps near Gordonsville, Virginia, on May 5, they had hustled 27 miles to the raging combat  in the Wilderness, where they arrived shortly after dawn on May 6 to save Lee's collapsing right flank. Longstreet then moved some of the men around the Federal left and coordinated an audacious flank attack and frontal assault. After Longstreet fell wounded, they continued fighting for the rest of the afternoon, sometimes in a maelstrom of blazing earthworks. When the attacks petered out, the First Corps hunkered down in the late afternoon for 24 hours of pot-shotting with their Federal counterparts.

Then, just after dark on May 7, they were roused again, this time from their positions in the burning forest for their move southward toward Spotsylvania. After their all-night march, and just a few miles away from their objective, Anderson finally allowed them to break—but with barely enough time to rest their feet, and with the sound of battle growing louder in the east, Fitz Lee's message had arrived to rouse them again.

"Field's Division, which was leading and which by this time was pretty well closed up, resumed the march immediately at double quick," explained Anderson in his later report. The division moved east along Shady Grove Church Road and across Block House Bridge before

Maj. Gen. Jeb Stuart (inset)

The southernmost part of Spindle field, between the Confederate line and the ridgeline where Sarah Spindle's house sat

23

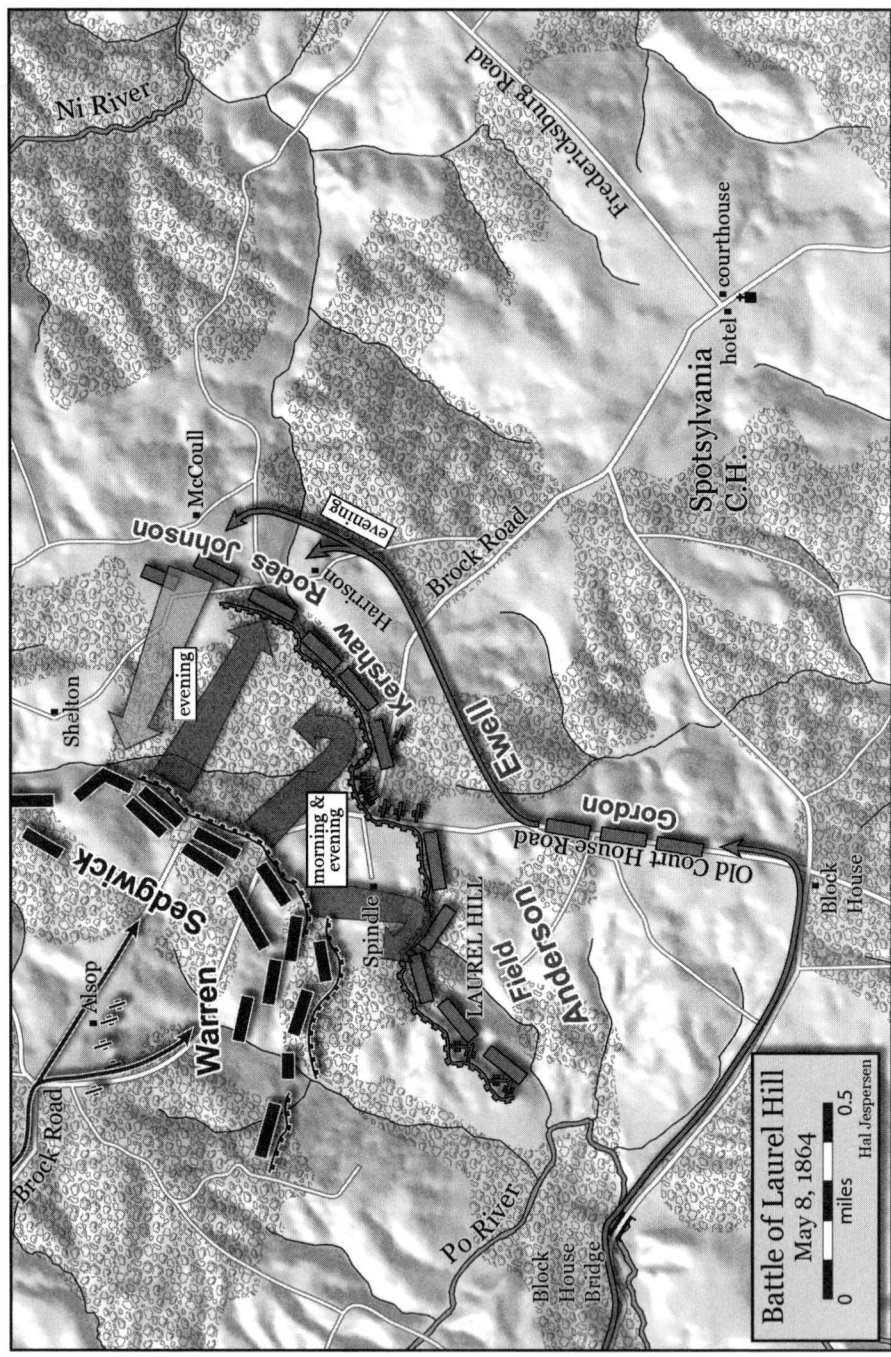

Battle of Laurel Hill
May 8, 1864

0   miles   0.5

Hal Jespersen

Battle of Laurel Hill

As Confederate infantry arrived on the field, they funneled into place just in time to bottleneck the Federals, who made piecemeal attacks up the Brock Road and across Spindle field. The arrival of reinforcements later in the day did nothing to break the impasse, although Federals did briefly penetrate the Southern works.

As Confederates strengthened their position, they took advantage of the terrain, following a ridgeline as they extended their line to the northeast. Eventually, their line would bulge outward in a horseshoe shape.

Fighting along Laurel Hill

swinging north onto Old Court House Road. Field's men finally reached Laurel Hill just before 8:00 a.m.

For a second time in three days the men of First Corps arrived at exactly the right place at exactly the right time.

"Run for our rail piles," Jeb Stuart told them as he directed the men into line. "The Federal infantry will reach them first, if you don't run."

Following the contour of the ridgeline, Stuart first anchored Col. John Henagan's South Carolina brigade on the left side of the Brock Road, placing one regiment in the road itself at the intersection where Old Court House Road split away. Stuart extended the line to the northeast by anchoring Brig. Gen. Benjamin Humphries' Mississippi brigade to the right of Brock Road. Confederate artillery also rolled into battery atop the hill.

"Hold your fire until the federals are well within range and then give it to them and hold this position to the last man," Stuart ordered. "Plenty of help is near at hand."

It was one of Stuart's finest days of the war, rivaled only by his leadership of the Confederate Second Corps at Chancellorsville on May 3, 1863, when he stepped in for the fallen Stonewall Jackson. In both instances, Lee's fabled cavalry commander led infantry—not horsemen—into battle.

Anderson, so impressed by Stuart that he offered to turn over field command, marveled at the work. "As fast as the other troops of Longstreet's Corps came up they were pushed rapidly to the support of Field's Division," he wrote, seeming to forget that it was actually his corps now, not Longstreet's, "and they maintained their positions until Lee arrived with the main body of his army."

But even as his men filed up the backside of Laurel Hill and into position, Anderson faced another crisis. Word came from Spotsylvania Court House that a full division of Federal cavalry had pushed into the village and was making for the Confederate rear. Without hesitation, Fitz Lee dispatched a cavalry regiment to slow the threat; Anderson dispatched Brig. Gen. Joseph Kershaw's division to back the troopers up.

Union cavalry under Brig. Gen. James Wilson tried approaching the Confederate position from behind but met with unexpected resistance.

The Union cavalry in town was the woefully undersized division of Brig. Gen. James Wilson, thinned by a reorganization of the cavalry the month before. Wilson had already bungled once at the start of the campaign: his inexperience as a cavalry commander had allowed the Confederates to approach the Wilderness virtually undetected on May 5. Now, days later, Wilson looked to redeem himself with bold action. He and his men had made an end run into Spotsylvania Court House from the east, where they then struck north along the Brock Road, heading right for the Confederates from behind.

Although Wilson's men posed a legitimate threat, they had entirely isolated themselves from the rest of the Army of the Potomac. Wilson recognized his vulnerability. As quickly as he had arrived, Wilson—with a great deal of coaxing from Anderson's infantry—pulled out of town.

Had Wilson pressed his attack, with Maj. Gen. Gouverneur K. Warren's entire V Corps pressing from the front, the battle of Spotsylvania might have lasted just a single day. Instead, it would drag on for two and a half weeks.

* * *

Although Wilson did not press his attack, Warren did—but not knowing exactly what he was up against, he didn't press with enough vigor. "We must drive them from there, or they will get some artillery in position," he said, still convinced that only cavalry stood in their way. From his position in the rear, he urged his men forward.

Meanwhile, his lead division—Robinson's—began to falter against the stiffening Confederate resistance. Already exhausted by their pursuit of Fitz Lee's cavalry, Robinson's brigades began to stack up against each other, making it difficult for them to deploy effectively. The best Robinson could do was send the brigades in one at a time as they arrived on the scene.

The five regiments of Col. Peter Lyle's brigade led the way, deploying on the eastern side of Brock Road. To Lyle's right, the men of Col. Andrew Denison's all-Maryland Brigade formed up. Extending Robinson's line southwest was a brigade borrowed from Brig. Gen. Charles Griffin's division. Robinson's final brigade, in turn, would come on line with the rest of Griffin's division.

From the Federal position, Laurel Hill rose in a gentle open slope toward a ridge capped by a home owned by Sarah Spindle. Beyond the Spindle home, but out of view from the Federal vantage point, the open field dipped away and then rose again to the ridge occupied by the Southerners.

Maj. Gen. Gouverneur K. Warren, commander of the Union V Corps

From the perspective of the ridge where Sarah Spindle's house once sat, looking back down across the open rise that Union soldiers had to advance across. The entrance to the modern battlefield park sits where the converging lines of trees meet along the far edge of the field.

"Confederate troops can be seen working like beavers felling abatis of small pine trees," a Massachusetts soldier said.

As soon as Robinson's men strode into the open ground of the Spindle field, Confederates opened on them.

One tired Federal division stood little chance of breaching the bolstered Confederate line, but Robinson's men did what they could. Lyle's men "zealously charge, amid artillery and small arms fire, and running, jump over a rail fence, stopping within 30' of the Confederate works," a Federal soldier wrote as if in the moment. Officers and men fell by the scores—including Robinson, his left knee shattered by a ball.

The Mississippians on Lyle's front extended their line well past their adversaries and began enfilading the right flank of Robinson's entire division. "[T]here was but one course to take," realized a Federal infantryman, "and our retreat was immediately made in the greater confusion."

By 9:00 a.m., the bulk of Robinson's men were making their way back across Spindle field. "The sun was so hot, and the men so exhausted from the long run as well as from the five days and nights of fighting and marching, that this retreat, though disorderly, was exceedingly slow, and we lost heavily in consequence from the enemy's fire," one Federal recalled.

Brig. Gen. John Robinson

The V Corps had plenty of resources to bring to the fight at Laurel Hill but could not bring everything to bear at once.

Fortunately, Union artillery, which had finally joined the fight, provided at least some cover. "[T]he breastworks of the two lines had been run very close together and each gun seemed discharging its contents into the throat of another," one Confederate artillerist remembered.

Warren fed more troops into the fray. Hardnosed, tough-as-nails Charles Griffin led his veteran division to the front. They came on line to the right of Robinson's division, but because of the massive Federal traffic jam along Brock Road—not to mention Warren's stubborn misperception about what was really going on—Griffin's men were unable to add their full weight to Robinson's initial assault.

By the time they went in alone, Griffin's men fared little better than Robinson's. The most successful was Brig. Gen. Joseph Bartlett, whose brigade went in with Robinson's initial assault. Bartlett's men made it to the improvised Confederate works, and at least two of his regiments—the 44th New York and 83rd Pennsylvania, known collectively as the "Potomac Blues"—momentarily mounted them. Due to Warren's haste, however, no reinforcements were at hand to exploit the momentary breakthrough, and Bartlett was repulsed.

Following Bartlett's repulse, the remainder of Robinson's and Griffin's men finally came on line. By this time, two more Confederate brigades had done the same. More Federals assaults resulted in more repulses.

Warren's men pulled off the heights.

* * *

Warren himself remained undaunted. He called upon his remaining two divisions, those of surgeon-turned-Brig. Gen. Samuel Crawford and Brig. Gen. Lysander Cutler. Crawford's division consisted of the Pennsylvania Reserves, which had once been one of the finest divisions in the Army of the Potomac. By now, though, the Reserves were a former shell of themselves, their best and brightest left behind on the

Richmond Peninsula, in the Cornfield of Antietam, and along the slopes of Prospect Hill at nearby Fredericksburg. Most of the rest of the division was due for discharge in a month, which meant they had little interest in fighting. The Reserves did their duty, though—but no more—and in Warren's second full assault, at 10:45 a.m., they were thrust back.

In Cutler's division, it was much the same. Cutler had just ascended to command on May 6, taking over for the popular millionaire general James Wadsworth, mortally wounded and captured by Confederates in the Wilderness. Cutler's division included such vaunted units as the Iron Brigade and Bucktail Brigade. Like their Reserve counterparts, the Iron Brigade had left many of their best and brightest on the fields of Antietam, but their heaviest losses came in Herbst Woods at Gettysburg. The Bucktails, meanwhile, had suffered worst around the Edward McPherson farm at Gettysburg.

The Wilderness had been a thoroughly humiliating affair for the entire division, which had twice been driven from the field. Their third route in three days lay ahead in Spindle field. Cutler advanced his men across the open ground as far as humanly possible, but overwhelming Confederate fire forced them back.

* * *

George Meade, in a rage, believed the V Corps' piecemeal attacks actually reflected a loss of nerve on Warren's part. He ordered Warren to call off the assaults—offending the V Corps commander—until reinforcements

Warren rallies the Marylanders.

arrived from Maj. Gen. John Sedgwick's VI Corps—offending Warren even more. Because of the infernal snarl on the Brock Road, though, Sedgwick's men had to take a roundabout route to reach the front, which didn't bring them into line until mid afternoon.

By that time, the full weight of Anderson's First Corps was on the field, with elements of Lt. Gen. Richard Ewell's Second Corps arriving, as well. The delay gave Confederates time to improve their works, which would make any renewed Federal assault that much harder. Meade sent his aide, Theodore Lyman, to urge things along.

"A little below where road opens into an extensive open space, [I] found Gens. Sedgwick, Warren & Wright," Lyman later recalled. "Was struck by their worn and troubled aspect, more especially in Sedgwick, who showed its effect more from contrast with his usual calmness."

In fact the sudden transition from a long winter's rest to hard marching, sleepless nights, and protracted fighting, with no prospect of cessation, produced a powerful effect on the nervous system of the whole army. And never, perhaps, were officers and men more jaded and prostrated than on this very Sunday . . . Gen. Sedgwick said 'Where is the Vermont Brigade? Not up yet—just when I wanted it—everything unlucky!' Neither he nor Warren could give no positive answer when they would assault.

Meade's worst fears about the two subordinates seemed to crystalize in that moment. He had earlier accused Warren of losing his nerve, and he believed Sedgwick "constitutionally slow." So, when he ordered the assault, he didn't specifically articulate who should be in command. Perhaps he felt he didn't need to: by virtue of seniority, the task should fall to Sedgwick, and that was at least implied when he cut Warren's orders, which said "cooperate with Sedgwick."

The vain Warren wanted no part of such an arrangement. "I'll be damned if I'll cooperate with Sedgwick or anybody else," Warren seethed in his letter back to Meade. "You are the commander of this army and can give the orders and I will obey them; or you can put Sedgwick in command and he can give the orders and I will obey them; or you can put me in command and I will give the orders and Sedgwick will obey them; but I'll be God Damned if I will cooperate with General Sedgwick or anybody else."

This wasn't Meade's only major conflict with a subordinate that day. Around noon, his chief of cavalry, "Little Phil" Sheridan, had come storming into headquarters. "I found [Meade's] peppery temper had got the better of his good judgment, he showing a disposition to be unjust, laying blame here and there for the blunders that had been committed. He was particularly severe on the cavalry," Sheridan said rather defensively in his memoirs. Truth was, his cavalry had underperformed badly during the entire campaign, and their latest failure had cost the army its chance to beat the Confederates into Spotsylvania. Grant had expected Meade and the army to be through the Court House by now and well on its way to the North Anna River to the south, not bottled up where it was.

Warren had been caught in the middle of the tangle. His men were the ones who'd discovered Sheridan's sleeping troopers at Todd's Tavern, and Warren himself had confronted Sheridan about the snarl. It was the first clash in an ongoing feud between the two generals that would eventually end in Warren's dismissal, at Sheridan's hand, in early April 1865 during the battle of Five Forks outside Petersburg.

As Sheridan and Meade had at each other, "[o]ne word brought on another," Sheridan recalled. "Meade was very much irritated, and I was none the less so . . ."

> [F]inally, I told him that I could whip Stuart if he (Meade) would only let me, but since he insisted on giving the cavalry directions without consulting or even notifying me, he could henceforth command the Cavalry Corps himself—that I would not give it another order.

Meade tried to strike a more conciliatory tone, but Sheridan stormed out. Flabbergasted by such insubordination, the army commander could do nothing about it because of Sheridan's favored status with Grant.

So Meade appealed to the General-in-Chief directly, repeating Sheridan's assertion that he could whip Stuart. "Did Sheridan say so?" Grant replied. "Well, he generally knows what he is talking about. Let him start right out and do it."

Meade suddenly found himself without his cavalry at just the time he would need them most.

* * *

As the afternoon wore on, Sedgwick's corps filed onto the battlefield, extending the Federal battle line to the north and east. Like their V Corps counterparts, the men of the Greek Cross had endured a drawn-out march over oppressively hot and dusty roads. Not until 6:15 p.m. was the assault force ready to move forward—with Warren in command thanks to good-natured placating by Sedgwick.

"[T]HE SUDDEN TRANSITION FROM A LONG WINTER'S REST TO HARD MARCHING, SLEEPLESS NIGHTS, AND PROTRACTED FIGHTING, WITH NO PROSPECT OF CESSATION, PRODUCED A POWERFUL EFFECT ON THE NERVOUS SYSTEM OF THE WHOLE ARMY."

Laurel Hill, like much of the land around Spotsylvania Court House, was far more open than the tangled forest of the Wilderness. Grant hoped the open space would give the army room to maneuver. Lee bottled him up, anyway.

Across a nearly one-mile front, 10,000 Union soldiers pushed across the open field. They made it all the way to the Confederate line. "We cut them down dreadfully," a VI Corps soldier said. "The ground was covered with the dead and dieing. They laid like sheaves of wheat in a harvest field."

Pockets of Federals even achieved breakthroughs. "Front, rear and flanks were lost in the whirl," one of them said; "organization was gone; each man depended upon himself; darkness increased the confusion and the result hung upon personal tenacity."

"Men fought with desperation," recalled one regiment's historian:

> *Hungered, fatigued, discouraged, they were goaded to a frenzied madness. Hand-to-hand conflicts were numerous bayonets crossed frequently; muskets were clubbed repeatedly. Swords clashed and revolvers that had never left their holsters to be discharged in anger were freely used. Shouts, yells, imprecations, heard above the noise of battle, were incessant. Alone, a mile beyond relief, menaced by death or captivity, the men were in a mood to fight and fight hard.*

But once more, Confederate reinforcements arrived at the right place at the right time. Major General Edward "Allegheny" Johnson's division extended the Confederate right and threw back the Union assaults.

"Slowly the firing ceased . . ." one Confederate said. "The dead, for the time, and in many instances perhaps for all time, were left undisturbed where they lay."

At Laurel Hill

The best way to see Laurel Hill is to park at the Spotsylvania Battlefield exhibit shelter and follow the path along the right side of Grant Drive that leads out to Spindle field. On the far side of the Brock Road, a trail 1.2 miles long skirts the edge of the field. Hikers should please use caution crossing Brock Road (Route 613) because cars tend to speed along this stretch. Also, there's no shade along the way, so it can be a particularly brutal walk in the full summer sun. Hikers should be sure to take water.

The trail dips into a shallow depression, which gets steeper as the field goes farther west, and then rises to the ridge where Sarah Spindle's house once stood. A farm lane now tops the ridge's crest. Only here can someone see that the field continues on for another 150 yards—a topographical feature hidden by the ridge. The path continues across the extra section of field before running into the woodline where Jeb Stuart and Richard Anderson had placed the troops of the First Corps.

Also in the woodline stands a monument for the Maryland Brigade, which penetrated the Confederate line. After a fierce hand-to-hand fight, surging Confederate numbers pushed the Marylanders back. It was the farthest advance any Federal unit made up Laurel Hill during the entire occupation of Spotsylvania.

The Maryland Brigade monument at Laurel Hill sits just inside the southern treeline.

Colonel Charles Phelps of the 7th Maryland installed the monument, with no apparent fanfare, shortly after he bought the property in 1885 for that expressed purpose. Phelps had led the Maryland Brigade after its colonel, Andrew Denison, fell wounded. Phelps was wounded, in turn, and captured during the hilltop melee. His gallantry earned him the Medal of Honor, though, and a brevet promotion to brigadier general.

⟶ FROM STOP 3A BACK TO STOP 3

Once you've completed the loop across Spindle Field, return to the VI Corps monument to Sedgwick located on park property near the intersection of Brock Road and Grant Drive. Be mindful of traffic as you cross Brock Road.

GPS: N 38° .21908 W 77° .61420

"The Death of "Uncle John" Sedgwick

CHAPTER FIVE

MAY 9, 1864

His men called him "Uncle John." Major General John Sedgwick, commander of the Union VI Corps, was as beloved by his troops as any man in the Army of the Potomac. The 50-year-old bachelor, good-natured, with a salt-and-pepper beard sharpened to a point, was so well

liked that even Robert E. Lee thought of him warmly. "Major Sedgwick," Lee called him, out of habit perhaps, from their prewar days when they had been friends and Sedgwick still wore oak leaves. Now, as one of the most senior officers in the army, Uncle John was practically the grand old man of the Army of the Potomac.

Sedgwick had served his entire career in the military. After graduating from West Point with the Class of 1837, he worked his way through the ranks with service in the Seminole Wars, the Mexican War, and the Mormon conflicts out west. By the time the Civil War erupted, Sedgwick was a lieutenant colonel, and he made brigadier general by August of 1861, although he missed the battle of First Manassas in July of that year because of a bout of cholera. He ably led his men during service on the Peninsula, but at the battle of Antietam, he led them into a withering hail of lead in the West Woods, where he was knocked out of action with wounds to his wrist, shoulder, and leg.

Sedgwick returned to service in late December of that year as the army tried to recover from its devastating defeat in Fredericksburg. During the Chancellorsville campaign, he provided one of the few bright spots for the Army of the Potomac with a win at the battle of Second Fredericksburg, although he was quickly bottled up at Salem Church and forced to retreat. At Gettysburg a few months later,

Maj. Gen. "Uncle John" Sedgwick (inset)

The Sedgwick monument at Spotsylvania

As a soldier's officer, Sedgwick made it a point to sleep under the stars like his men.

his corps was the last to arrive on July 2, missing most of the significant action. His high point may have come in November when his corps punched through Confederate defenses at the battle of Rappahannock Station.

"Sedgwick was essentially a soldier," wrote one of Grant's staffers. "He had never married; the camp was his home, and the members of his staff were his family." His men loved him. He was "one of the truest and whitest souls ever known to any army," one of them said.

Gouverneur Warren, by contrast, was prickly at the best of times, and he had bristled when Sedgwick arrived the day before, appearing on the scene as though Warren needed his fat pulled from the Laurel Hill fire. Sedgwick did his best to soothe the younger man's wounded ego, though, and suggested better days lay ahead.

Making camp on the edge of Sarah Spindle's field, Sedgwick slept under the stars, which was his habit while on campaign. He cozied up near a hay bale.

"We laid on our arms all night," a nearby Ohioan said, "and at early dawn set about felling some trees, and building breastworks. The boys worked with a will, and soon had quite a formidable line erected in our front. The rebel sharp shooters hid in the thick tree tops annoyed us very much, and every now and then some man was struck by them."

Sedgwick spent the morning of May 9 receiving the daily reports of his officers, bantering with his staff, and overseeing the improvement of the Federal earthworks. He "seemed particularly cheerful and hopeful that morning, and looked the picture of buoyant life and vigorous health," one of Grant's staffers later noted.

After 36 hours of marching and fighting, Sedgwick expected the day to be relatively calm. "The army will remain quiet . . ." Meade had ordered the evening before, "to give the men rest and to distribute ammunition and rations."

Orders or not, the day was hardly quiet. Pickets and sharpshooters traded sporadic firing along the line, which kept everyone edgy. Wounded men still littered the no-man's land of Spindle field between the armies. "They could be heard to call out for water and seen to move and throw up their hands, and one in particular would sometimes sit up," one soldier said. "[T]here was nothing left for those men but to die there."

Both sides strengthened their positions. Warren's V Corps fanned out to either side of the Brock Road. Sedgwick's VI Corps extended the line to the left. Major General Winfield Scott Hancock's II Corps hung back near Todd's Tavern as a reserve.

The concentration left too much of the army dependent on a choked transportation network, though. To alleviate the clog, General-in-Chief Grant directed Maj. Gen. Ambrose Burnside's IX Corps to move on a side road that took him well east of Sedgwick, with orders to find a way into Spotsylvania Court House from the north.

*   *   *

Across Spindle field, Lee's army continued to fortify its position as well. During the night, as more elements of the army arrived on the field, Lee's chief engineer, Maj. Gen. Martin Luther Smith, oversaw their deployment. Following the contours of the land, he directed the infantry to extend the line northeast from Laurel Hill along a low ridge.

However, when morning arrived and Lee got a clearer look at his army's position, he recognized an inherent weakness: the line formed a salient.

A salient is akin to a large bubble that juts outward from a defensive position. This bubble can be bombarded from three sides, exposing defenders inside to converging artillery fire. This concentration of artillery can hit defenders in the front, flank, or rear. One Virginian "in the toe of the shoe" said his fellow soldiers recognized the

An aluminum sign once posted at the Bloody Angle shows the bulge in the Confederate line that became known as the Mule Shoe. The sign depicts the action of May 12, 1864.

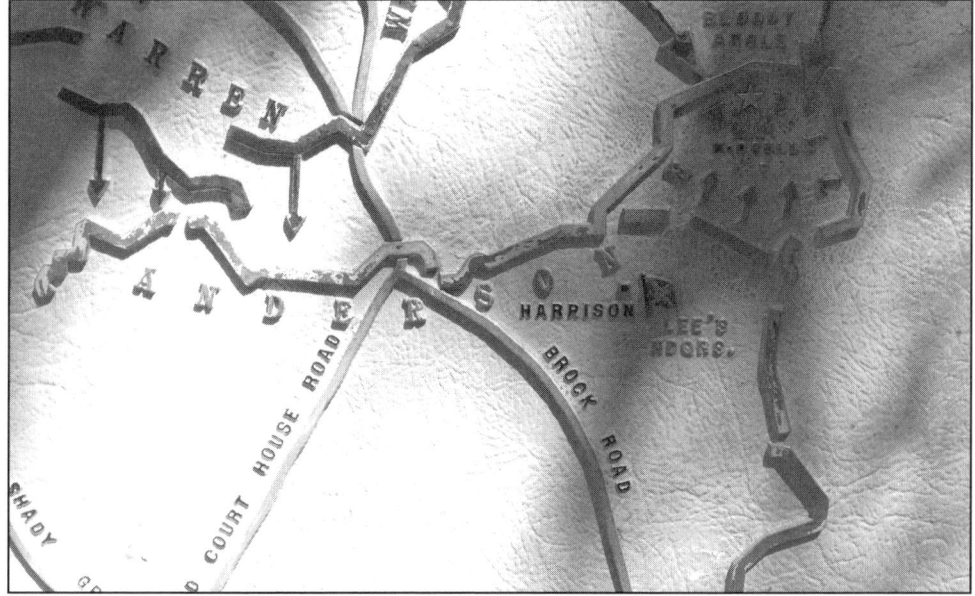

danger and tried their best to protect themselves from it. "After throwing up breastworks, we found that the Yanks had a cross fire on our regiment," he said. "We then went to work and built pens, each holding eight or ten men." The pens offered extra protection.

Defenders firing outward from a salient employ diverging artillery fire—their firepower fans out from the bubble, rather than concentrating, thus diluting the firepower's effectiveness. Finally, a salient can be "popped" if attackers hit the bubble's base from the side or an assault comes at its tip.

The Confederate salient was, one soldier lamented, "a bad piece of engineering and certain to invite attack as soon as the enemy understood it."

A salient does offer one significant advantage, however: the interior lines make it easier to move troops from one point to another. In fact, a Boston journalist who saw the army's position made a foreboding comparison. "The lines were in a form of a horseshoe," he reported. "It was Gettysburg reversed—Lee having the inner circle."

Because of that shoe shape, the Confederate position became known as the Mule Shoe Salient.

Lieutenant General Richard Ewell's Second Corps occupied the salient. Lee conferred with Ewell about the position, recognizing its vulnerability. However, in its favor, the Mule Shoe enclosed a piece of high ground that Federals could otherwise use as an artillery platform to bombard any Confederate line farther back. Keeping it inside Confederate lines protected it.

The Mule Shoe, said one Confederate brigadier, was "a point which with artillery was strong, but without it weak." Ewell shared that assessment, and he assured Lee he could defend the position so long as he had enough artillery to support his men. Lee let the position stand.

Beyond Ewell, Lee's Third Corps extended the Confederate line eastward across the Fredericksburg Road, blocking any approach Federals might have toward Spotsylvania Court House. Due to the terrain, not all of the corps was needed on line, which allowed Lee to hold two full divisions as a mobile reserve.

The Third Corps, as it happened, found itself under temporary new leadership. Major General Jubal Early—"Lee's Bad Old Man," who had been in consideration for the First Corps command that ended up going to Dick Anderson—had been tapped to take over for an ailing Lt. Gen. A. P. Hill. Hill, who suffered the chronic effects of a "social disease" he'd contracted years earlier as a West Point cadet, suffered an acute flair-up that forced him to relinquish command. Lee had already just lost Longstreet, so Hill's loss came at a time when Lee could ill afford it.

However, the Union army was about to experience turnover among senior leadership, too.

*   *   *

Midway between Todd's Tavern and Laurel Hill, Brock Road split in two, and the legs bowed away from each other before rejoining at the edge of Spindle field, at Laurel Hill's base. Federals had placed an artillery battery at the intersection, but Confederate sharpshooters harassed the officers and the men of the battery relentlessly and harassed the infantrymen supporting the battery, too. As frontline troops shuffled into new positions throughout the early morning, some of the infantry blocked the field of fire of one of those guns. Uncle John decided to rectify the situation.

Sedgwick had moved toward the intersection once already during the morning, but his chief of staff, Col. Martin T. "Mac" McMahon, pulled him back. McMahon recalled the incident after the war:

> *I had remarked to the general, pointing to the two pieces in a half-jesting manner, which he [Sedgwick] well understood, 'General do you see that section of artillery? Well you are not to go near it today.'*
>
> *He answered good naturedly, 'McMahon I would like to know who commands this corps, you or I?'*
>
> *I said playfully, 'Well, General, sometimes I am in doubt myself'; added, 'Seriously, General, I beg you not to go to that angle; every officer who has shown himself there has been hit, both yesterday and today.'*
>
> *He answered quietly, 'Well, I don't know that there is any reason for my going there.'*

But after an hour or so, Sedgwick apparently forgot McMahon's admonition. He moved to the front and began reshuffling his men. The increased activity kicked up a

The death of "Uncle John" Sedgwick

flurry of sharpshooting from the Confederates. While the men around him ducked and dived, Sedgwick didn't flinch. "What! What! Men, dodging this way for single bullets!" he joked. "What will you do when they open fire along the whole line? I am ashamed of you. They couldn't hit an elephant at this distance."

A bullet whistled by, and a soldier near Sedgwick dodged away from the sound. Sedgwick chuckled at him. "Why, my man, I am ashamed of you, dodging that way," the general said. He repeated his earlier assertion, "They couldn't hit an elephant at this distance."

The man saluted the general and told him how dodging a shell once had saved his life. Sedgwick laughed, then said, "Go to your place."

A moment later, the whistle of another bullet shot by— followed by a dull thud. Sedgwick turned to McMahon as if to say something, but blood poured out from underneath his left eye. The hefty general collapsed on his staff officer instead.

Sedgwick's chief of artillery witnessed what happened and immediately called for a surgeon, but it was too late. The bullet had killed Sedgwick instantly. By the time the surgeon arrived, all he could do was pour water on the general's wound, which created a small fountain of blood.

"We could not believe for a long time that our kind old leader had fallen but soon it was confirmed that he was indeed gone," one soldier said. "There is not a man in the 6th Corps but what mourns his loss, nor any one in the whole army for that matter."

"[W]e were perfectly astounded," a Pennsylvanian recalled. "[W]e knew he was reckless and brave, but the thought that he would be killed never occurred to us."

Sedgwick's replacement at the head of the VI Corps, Maj. Gen. Horatio Wright

*   *   *

Even as events with Sedgwick unfolded at the front, Winfield Scott Hancock got word that he could vacate his position near Todd's Tavern. Through aggressive cavalry work, Confederate cavalryman Wade Hampton had frozen Hancock in place on May 8, effectively keeping him out of the fight at Laurel Hill. The hard-fighting Hancock was only too glad to now get back into the action.

Orders directed his men south down the Brock Road and then west for the Po River. Hancock was to find a fordable point and cross three of his four divisions to the far bank. Then they were to skirt the river and attempt to re-cross at Block House Bridge, taking the Confederates in the flank and rear. In support, the V and VI corps would assault Lee's men from the front. If all went well, Lee's army would be brushed aside and the door to the crossroads would be kicked open.

By the time Hancock moved into position, though, much of the afternoon had passed. He worried that if any of his men crossed, they'd be isolated and vulnerable to attack. With daylight running out, there might not be enough time for a rescue.

Meade and Grant were content to let things go for the day. The loss of Sedgwick had dampened their mood considerably. "His loss to this army is greater than the loss of a whole division of troops," Grant told an aide.

By virtue of seniority, command of VI Corps should have devolved to Brig. Gen. James Ricketts. However, Ricketts knew his dead commander wished to have Horatio Wright lead the corps in the event that anything ever happened. Manfully, the more-senior division commander stepped aside, and Meade promoted Wright.

Grant, meanwhile, already had his eye on tomorrow.

At the Spotsylvania Battlefield Exhibit Shelter

Sedgwick's monument was the first formal monument on any of the Fredericksburg/Spotsylvania battlefields. A quartz boulder marking the area of Stonewall Jackson's wounding at Chancellorsville may predate it.

The monument to John Sedgwick that sits near the entrance to the battlefield is the oldest formal monument in the entire Fredericksburg and Spotsylvania National Military Park (a quartz bolder placed near the spot of Stonewall Jackson's wounding at Chancellorsville may predate it). Former members of the Sixth Corps raised the money after visiting the battlefield in October of 1886 and decided that something should mark the spot where their beloved Uncle John had fallen. The monument was dedicated on May 12, 1887, the 23rd anniversary of the fighting at the Bloody Angle. Thousands of people turned out, including Sedgwick's successor, Horatio Wright.

"It was intended to put the stone on the very spot where the general fell," one correspondent reported, "and perhaps it is on that spot—but this is doubtful . . ."

But ordinary testimony on things that happened yesterday is never certain; and in locating within a few feet of an event that happened in the woods twenty-four years ago, one opinion is as good as another. For the far away friends in the North the monument is practically where the old soldier fell—for at such a distance a few feet do not count.

The granite monument stands nine feet tall with a base five and half feet square. "It is a solid and impressive design, in keeping with the strong and trustworthy character of the man it memorializes," another newspaperman wrote.

Also at the intersection stands an artillery piece. Artillerists posted here would have been under hot fire from Confederate sharpshooters, as Sedgwick's death demonstrated.

A stop at the nearby Spotsylvania Battlefield exhibit shelter offers a general overview of the battle—including pictures, maps, and testimonials from some of the participants—and restroom facilities. Near this spot, Peter Lyle's brigade lined up for its attack on Laurel Hill on May 8.

⟶ TO STOP 4

Turn left onto Grant Drive and follow it 0.6 miles to the pull-off for Upton's Road and park there.

Opposite: The spot where Sedgwick was shot now serves as the entrance to the battlefield

GPS: N 38° .22346 W 77° .60597

Upton's Attack

CHAPTER SIX

MAY 10, 1864

When Col. Emory Upton walked into the tent, Martin McMahon passed him a sheet of paper. The report listed twelve regiments—4,500 men—including Upton's own 121st New York.

"What do you think of that for a command?" the VI Corps' chief of staff asked.

"Mac, that is a splendid command," the colonel replied. "They are the best men in the army."

"Upton, you are to lead those men upon the enemy's works this afternoon—and if you do not carry them, you are not expected to come back," McMahon told him. "But if you carry them, I am authorized to say that you will get your stars."

"Mac," Upton said, "I will carry those works. If I don't, I won't come back."

The news elated Upton. Earlier in the day, he had put forward a new plan for assaulting the Confederate line. His idea made its way up the chain of command and, as evidenced by the list of regiments he now held in his hand, was approved.

The colonel hopped back on his horse. "I'll carry those works," he repeated. "They cannot repulse those regiments!"

Although just 24, Upton was already a rising star in the Army of the Potomac. A native of Batavia, New York, and a member of West Point's Class of 1861, Upton first served as an artillerist before assuming command of the 121st in late 1862. His regiment, dubbed "Upton's Regulars," was well disciplined and well drilled—a true reflection of their stern, tough-as-nails commander. A nearly humorless man, Upton took his duties as an officer seriously.

Col. Emory Upton (inset)

Where Upton's trail emerges from the woods, a monument now stands watch over the former attack field.

45

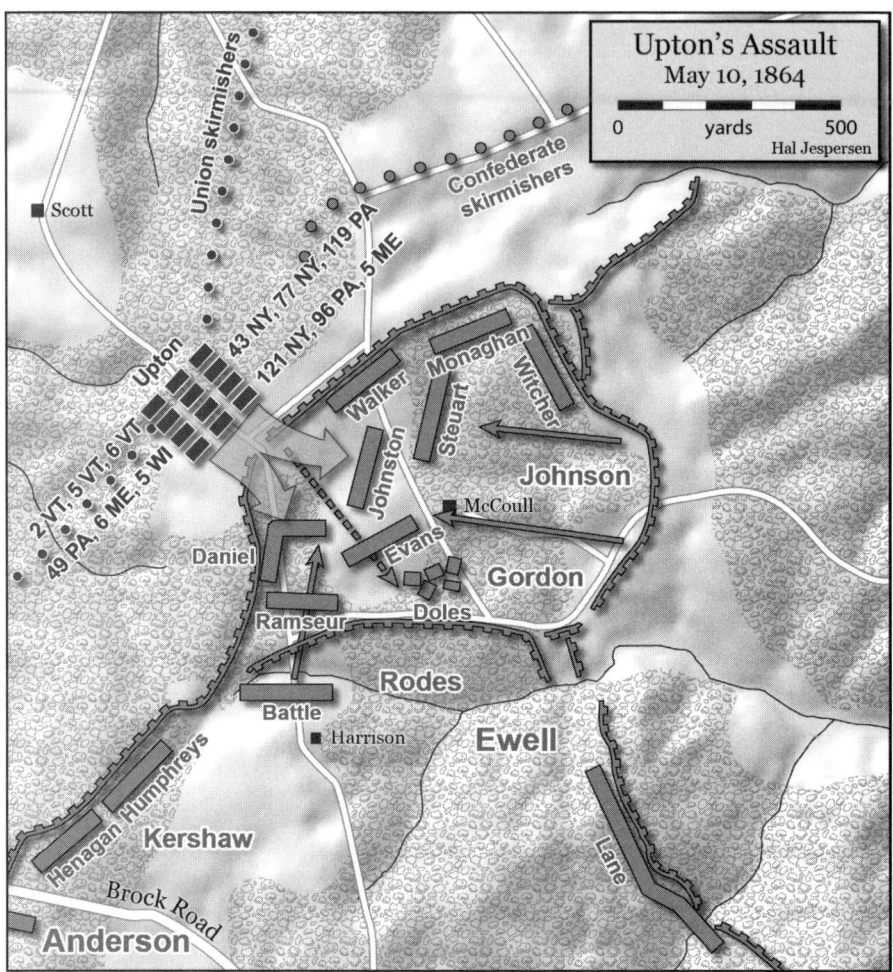

Upton's Assault
May 10, 1864

0 — yards — 500

Hal Jespersen

UPTON'S ASSAULT

After organizing his attack force into a column three regiments wide and four regiments deep, Upton charged them across 200 yards of open field to strike a hammer-like blow against Confederates under George Doles. Upton's first row breached the Confederate line; the second row widened the gap; the third pushed into the breach; the fourth served as reserve. As Confederate reinforcements rushed to the scene, Upton's unsupported men were forced to fall back.

Upton may have lacked social graces, but he was blessed with a gifted military mind. He had quickly tired of the massed frontal assaults that Grant continued to use to bludgeon Lee's army into submission, so he offered an alternative.

The previous May, at the battle of Second Fredericksburg, the 121st New York was among six regiments that overwhelmed Confederates along the Sunken Road by assaulting them in a relatively novel way. The troops attacked not in a traditional line of battle but in a narrow column that struck more like a fist than a wave. Many of the same regiments executed the maneuver again back in November at Rappahannock Station, forcing a Confederate withdrawal.

Now Upton suggested a similar assault against the Confederate line. Rather than advance in two ranks of battle a mile or so long, Upton proposed a narrow front only a few regiments across. Though the formation would lack width, it would be deep and so have power. By massing the formation as close to the enemy line as possible, the column could dash forward without stopping to fire and punch a hole in the Confederate position, much the way a modern bazooka bores through armored plating.

Upton's front was ideal for the attack: the Union and Confederate lines came closer together there than anywhere else. "The [Confederate] position was in an open field about 200 yards from a pine wood, through which a wood road led from our lines direct to the enemy's works," described a Union solider. Additionally, the approach from the Federal line was screened by a sloping hill that dropped off into the woods, which would allow Upton's men to get into position in secrecy.

The Confederate position became known as Doles' Salient, which bulged like a small bubble on the side of the larger Mule Shoe Salient. The entrenchments, Upton later said, "were of a formidable character with abatis in front and surrounded by heavy logs, underneath which were loop holes for musketry."

The salient was named after 29-year-old Brig. Gen. George Doles, whose four Georgia regiments held the line at that point. Although not a military man by training, Doles had blossomed into a fine combat leader. On his left, he was supported by a North Carolina brigade led by Brig. Gen. Junius Daniel. On his right was the famed "Stonewall Brigade."

As Upton plotted his assault on the position, he organized his twelve regiments into a compact column three regiments across and four deep that would charge in four waves. The first line consisted of Upton's old regiment, the 121st New York, the 96th Pennsylvania, and 5th Maine. Their job was to kick in the door using brute strength and the bayonet. The men in the first wave were to load their muskets but not put the percussion cap in place—which would prevent them from stopping to fire.

Once in the works, the men of the first wave were to wheel to the right and left, opening a hole in the line, which the second and third waves would exploit. Those waves consisted of the 49th Pennsylvania, 6th Maine, 5th Wisconsin, 43rd New York, 77th New York, and 119th Pennsylvania.

The fourth and final wave—the 2nd, 5th, and 6th Vermont—would hold back in reserve, used either to further exploit the gap or cover a possible retreat.

*   *   *

As promising as Upton's plan looked, it represented just one cog in Grant's larger machinations. Elsewhere,

Confederate Brig. Gen. George Doles

A monument along Upton's trail maps out the formation of the twelve regiments that took part in the assault.

Warren saw a chance to jump the gun and launched his attack early instead of attacking in concert with Upton.

he finally sent three of Hancock's II Corps divisions across the Po River as he'd planned to do the previous afternoon. Hancock realized the vulnerability of his men almost immediately, caught as they were on the far side of a winding river with steep banks. Any reinforcements he might expect would have to pull from the main battle line and then march across the Po via three temporary pontoon bridges laid by Federal engineers.

Lee countered Hancock's move with the two Third Corps divisions he kept as mobile reserves. By the time the first of them arrived on the field, however, two-thirds of Hancock's corps had already withdrawn back to the Federal side of the Po. Grant had dangled Hancock as bait and now pulled that bait away.

The Confederate shift convinced the Federal high command that the enemy line had a weak point somewhere. To find it, Grant ordered a general assault, set for 5:00 p.m., along the entire length of Lee's line. Warren's V and Wright's VI would attack at Laurel Hill. Two of Hancock's divisions would support Warren's right. Another stayed on the far side of the Po while his fourth assisted Wright with his assault and served as a link between the IX Corps and the Army of the Potomac.

Thanks to Warren's ego—inflated as it usually was and bruised as it had become by his embarrassing performance the day before—the Federal plan unraveled from the start.

It was becoming abundantly clear to Grant and Meade that they could not trust Warren with important command decisions, so Grant placed Hancock in command of the assaults at Laurel Hill. However, the haughty Warren did not take kindly to playing second fiddle to Hancock any more than he'd wanted to play second to Sedgwick the day before. So, when an opportunity presented itself to attack without Hancock looking over his shoulder, Warren took it.

Hancock's attention had been diverted back across

The Upton Attack trail

the Po, where his isolated division suddenly found itself in danger of annihilation. To help, Hancock shifted another division to the river crossing and personally oversaw the action. Both divisions eventually withdrew to safety.

With Hancock out of the way, Warren informed headquarters that he saw a weakness in the Confederate front. At 3:30 p.m., fully an hour and a half before Grant's grand offensive, Warren ordered V Corps, a portion of II Corps left behind by Hancock, and part of VI Corps against Laurel Hill.

Once more, men apprehensively advanced into the open fields, and once more, their adversaries mowed them down. Warren failed to carry his objective.

*   *   *

While Warren went early, Upton ran late. His twelve regiments followed a narrow path that meandered through the woods from the Scott farm toward the Confederate line. Upton's men had to move as quietly as possible, so the march went slower than expected.

Upton's support, meanwhile—an undersized II Corps division commanded by Brig. Gen. Gershom Mott—attacked right on schedule at 5:00 p.m. Mott's two brigades served as the link between the IX Corps, farther to the east, and the rest of the army. In conjunction with Upton's assault, they were to apply pressure to the tip of the Mule Shoe where they would hopefully breach the Confederate line or, at worst, tie down reinforcements that might otherwise be sent to repel Upton.

Mott's men came across the open fields and pushed toward the Confederate picket line, which alerted the main battle line. By the time Mott's formation marched into rifle range, Confederates were ready and let loose with volley after volley. It took less than 20 minutes for Mott's formation to fall into complete disarray.

Meanwhile on Upton's front at 5:00 p.m., a lone Federal battery opened on the Confederate works. The young colonel's assault column was to receive only 10 minutes of artillery support in the form of a pre-assault barrage, but because of his tardiness, the bombardment lasted for over an hour. By 6:10 p.m., two more batteries began playing on the enemy line. "The accuracy with which our gunners fire is wonderful," marveled one Vermonter. "I have seen one piece of the enemy's artillery opposite me turned completely over backwards carriage and all, by a solid shot from one of our guns in front of our regiment; it evidently hit the enemy's cannon square in the muzzle."

Confederate gunners complained, in turn, that their position for counter-battery fire "was anything but a good one."

* * *

Upton called his 12 regimental commanders together and explained the plan. "All of the officers were instructed to repeat the command 'forward' constantly, from the commencement of the charge till the works were carried," he later recounted. "No man was to stop and succor or assist a wounded comrade." With that, the officers returned to their units to prepare for the advance.

One Pennsylvania soldier described the moments before the assault. "We are lying low, and not a word is spoken above a whisper in our ranks," he said. "We see the duty we are expected to perform, and orders are quietly passed along the line in a whisper."

At 6:30 p.m., Upton's men burst from the tree line. Wilbur Fisk of the 2nd Vermont recalled the way the first wave

> *rushed ahead across the open field, to the enemy's works, while we cheered as lustily as we could to heighten the effect, and help create a panic among the enemy. How terribly the bullets swept that plain, and rattled like hailstones among the trees over our heads. The boys could not be restrained in*

"THIS TO ME WAS THE HARDEST DAY OF THE FIGHT."

their wild excitement, and without waiting for orders (for I certainly heard no order to 'halt', and I know of no one that did) they rushed in after the other brigade, and we drove the enemy from his first line of works.

"Make ready boys—they are charging!" one Georgian shouted. Confederate fire erupted.

"Quick as lightning a sheet of flame burst from the rebel line, and the leaden hail swept the ground over which the column was advancing, while the canister from the artillery came crashing through our ranks at every step," recalled Priv. Robert Westbrook of the 49th Pennsylvania. Added another Pennsylvanian: "Many a poor fellow fell pierced with rebel bullets before we reached the rifle pits . . . When those of us that were left reached the rifle pits we let them have it."

Upton described the melee atop the works:

Here occurred a deadly hand-to-hand conflict. The enemy sitting in their pits with pieces upright, loaded and with bayonets fixed, ready to impale the first who should leap over, absolutely refused to yield the ground. The first of our men who tried to surmount the works fell pierced through the head by musket-balls. Others, seeing the fate of their comrades, held their pieces at arms length and fired downward, while others poising their pieces vertically, hurled them down upon their enemy, pinning them to the ground . . .

The Stonewall Brigade, posted along this section of the Confederate line, watched as Upton's men charged across the open field to the left of their position. The brigade sat along a low, swampy section of line (notice the standing water).

51

Confederate prisoners were quickly herded to the rear.

Upton's first wave kicked in the door with perfection. Swinging to the right, they swept Confederates from the works and captured guns of the Richmond Howitzers. To the left, they rolled the line back for 200 yards, reaching the bottom of a small swale where fire from the Stonewall Brigade stopped their advance.

Then over the top came the second wave, pushing farther into the interior of the salient and making for a reserve line of earthworks. "The Yankees fought with unusual desperation, and where the artillery was, contended as stubbornly for it as though it was their own," a Southern soldier lamented.

Although Confederates surrendered by the scores, some prisoners still had fight left in them. "[A] rebel lieutenant, after passing to the rear, orders his men to pick up the guns that our dead and wounded have left on the field and fire on us from the rear," a Union soldier recalled. One of his comrades heard the order, he said, "and as quick as lighting he puts a ball into the rebel's back, who threw his hands up and dropped to the ground. This stopped the picking up of guns."

* * *

General Lee, for the second time in less than a week, rode out to rally his broken men. With cries of "Lee to the rear," wise Southern soldiers forced their commander to safety.

Second Corps commander Richard Ewell also rode to the front, his bravery conspicuous. "Don't run, boys," he bellowed. "I will have enough men here in five minutes to eat up every damned one of them!"

Ewell was true to his word. Into the fray charged the proud North Carolina brigade of Brig. Gen. Stephen Ramseur. From the far side of the Mule Shoe, more North Carolinians and Georgians also charged. These men began forcing the Yankee hordes back and sealing the gap behind them.

With his third line in the works, Upton rode back toward the tree line to find his fourth and final wave,

the Vermonters. He found the men already committed to the battle. They had moved up to the Confederate works and were firing on anything that moved, although Confederates still pressed in even closer. This did not deter the Vermonters. "We don't want to go," they told their commander. "Send us ammunition and rations, and we can stay here for six months." One newspaper correspondent observed, "The blood of the Green Mountain Boys was up and they absolutely refused to budge a single hair from the field they had wrested from the enemy."

Upton's corps commander, Horatio Wright, asked Grant for more men to send into the breach. "Pile in the men and hold it," Grant told him.

However, because of the Army of the Potomac's failure to coordinate a massed assault along the length of Lee's lines, Federals could not exert enough pressure to allow Upton to hold on. As determined as his men were, sheer numbers played against them. Confederates forced them from the works.

*   *   *

Along the tree line across from the salient, Federal doctors had set up an aid station. One of the surgeons, Dr. Daniel Holt, described the intense fire:

A very dusty time around my little flag, called a 'hospital'. Three times have I been shelled out and three times returned determined to hold my post but was compelled by outside pressure to yield to lead and powder arguments . . . Not less than three hundred and fifty wounded were sent to the rear . . . This to me was the hardest day of the fight. One man was shot a second time while in my arms dressing his wound, and expired.

Following the Union withdrawal from the salient, a Union officer recalled, a Confederate band moved up to an elevated position on the line. It played "Nearer My God to Thee." "The sound of this beautiful piece of music had scarcely died away when a Yankee band over the line gave us the 'Dead March.' This was closely followed by the Confederate band playing the 'Bonnie Blue Flag,'" Holt wrote. "As the last notes were wafted out on the crisp night air a grand old style rebel yell went up. The Yankee band then played 'The Star-Spangled Banner,' and . . . it seemed by the response yell, that every man in the Army of the Potomac was awake and listening to the music. The Confederate Band then rendered 'Home Sweet Home,' when a united yell went up in concert from the men on both sides."

Following the Civil War, Emory Upton stayed with the army and earned a reputation as one the great military thinkers of the 19th Century, influencing both military tactics and policy. He was sent on a trip of Europe and Asia to study their armies, structures, and tactics, then came back to the United States and wrote about his travels. In reporting his findings and his recommended changes, he helped predict the United States' involvement in future wars with Germany and Japan. By 1881, Upton was serving at the Presidio in California. He was, by that time, severely depressed over the death of his young wife and also suffered from intense migraines. He traveled the country looking for cures, including the early use of electroshock therapy. On March 15, 1881, he sat at his desk, wrote out his resignation letter, then drew his revolver from a drawer and shot himself in the head.

For nearly an hour, in a great feat of strength and ingenuity, Upton's 12 regiments had clung onto the Confederate works. Federals bagged 913 enlisted Confederates and 37 officers. More importantly to Grant, Upton's assault had demonstrated the weakness in Lee's line and what innovation could bring if employed on a larger scale. For Upton's actions Grant promoted him to brigadier general.

"The only battle to compare with Upton's Charge of May 10th, 1864, is Pickett's Charge at Gettysburg," one Federal soldier said. What Grant next had in store for the Army of the Potomac would make both charges pale in comparison.

At the Trail to Upton's Attack

The modern trailhead for Upton's Attack leads to the historic roadbed about one hundred feet into the forest, at the bottom of a gentle slope.

From the pull-off along Grant Drive, a path leads into the forest and intersects with the farm path Emory Upton's men took through the woods. Where the path reaches the bottom of its first downward stretch and turns left, a hiker can look to the right and see traces of the original roadbed, about six feet wide, that runs as a shallow depression under the leaf cover.

The ridge that the path winds its way upward provided perfect cover for Upton's men as they assembled into formation. Well off to the left, they might have heard the cannon fire that raked Gersham Mott's division when it stepped off at the appointed 5:00 hour, although the thick tree cover and low ground might have muffled some of it. Otherwise, it's hard to explain why Upton apparently didn't seem concerned that his support had started moving without him.

Farther up the path, just before it breaks into the open, a few depressions pock the ground. These are the remains of rifle pits—early forerunners of the modern foxhole—dug by Confederate pickets. The tree line is about 30 yards closer to the Confederate line today than it was in 1864, so the rifle pits would have been just inside the tree line. A few old roadbeds also criss-cross the area, although they're remnants of a different occupation: the 1930s Civilian Conservation Corps camp (see Appendix D). Others are the remnants of old logging roads. At the turn of the 19th century, a logging business operated in the area; the mill sat in the woods to the northeast of Doles' Salient.

Outside the modern tree line stands a flat obelisk that memorializes the 12 regiments that comprised Upton's attack force. On the opposite side, the monument lists the Confederate regiments stationed in Doles' Salient. The monument was dedicated in 1994.

Moving across the open space toward the Confederate line, a hiker can see how dramatically the terrain varies

The guns of the Richmond Howitzers mark the farthest advance of Upton's men.

from right to left. The regiments who crossed to the right of the path had a great deal of protection from the land itself because of the steep bowl soldiers had to come up out of. To the left, the field flattens out and even gets marshy in the low area closest to the park road, so attackers had far less protection.

The Confederate trenches today look like little more than humps of dirt, but in 1864, Confederates could stand in the fortifications. The wood has since rotted and the earthworks have collapsed in on themselves and wind and rain have eroded them to their poorly diminished state. To help preserve what's left, the Park Service allows plant life to grow on the earthworks; the root systems help keep the soil in place. At times, when the fields have grown up, the earthworks become difficult to see. The Park Service manages the fields through a careful combination of mowing and burning to knock the plant life back, but because of the fragility of the resources, the maintenance is performed only at certain times of the year.

Inside the Confederate lines, a few hundred yards to the right, two cannons sit alongside the road. These represent the guns that belonged to the Virginia Howitzers. When the artillerists saw Upton's men swarming toward them, they couldn't turn the cannons on them for fear of hitting their own men. Instead, they hopped over the earthworks and ran along the outside of the fortifications, finding shelter with the next battery farther down the line.

Across the road from the Richmond Howitzer's artillery pieces are the remains of a type of earthworks known as traverses. Built perpendicular to the main line, they were intended as fallback points in the event of a breakthrough. These traverses played a role in stopping Upton's advance. However, one reason Federals made it this far was because Confederates had not yet built enough traverses along this part of the line by May 10— a mistake they quickly rectified after repulsing Upton's breakthrough.

➡ TO STOP 5

Follow Grant Drive 0.3 miles to the Bloody Angle parking area, which will be on your left. Park there.

GPS: N 38° .22363 W 77° .60179

The First Day of Rain

CHAPTER SEVEN

MAY 11, 1864

"We have now ended the sixth day of very heavy fighting," the general-in-chief scribbled. "I propose to fight it out on this line if it takes all summer."

It was early in the day, but Grant, sitting at the writing table in his tent, was already chomping on a cigar. Of late, he'd taken to smoking as many as 20 a day—one of the few outwards signs that anything about the "heavy fighting" weighed on his nerves. His dispatch to Washington certainly showed little anxiety. "The result this time is much in our favor," he wrote.

It was the second time that morning he had offered that assessment. A few minutes before, he had told Congressman Elihu Washburne, "We are certainly making fair progress, and all the fighting has been in our favor." Washburne, a friend of Grant's and of Lincoln's, would take that message back to the president.

But Grant also knew "the campaign promises to be a long one," he told Washburne, and in his letter to Washington he confided, "our losses have been heavy as well as those of the enemy."

Grant entered the campaign knowing the grim arithmetic of war, and knew he had to keep grinding down Lee's army if he ever hoped to end the war. In that context, the failure of Upton's assault the day before represented only a minor setback. Grant had "but little doubt" Upton's assault "would have proved entirely successful" had it been better timed and better supported.

With those lessons in mind, Grant began to plan for a similar assault on a far grander scale. If Upton could score

Maj. Gen. Winfield Scott Hancock, "Hancock the Supurb" (inset)

Storm clouds gather over the Mule Shoe Salient.

a breakthrough with 4,500 men, what could Grant achieve with an entire corps?

To execute the plan, Grant called on the commander he had quickly come to depend on as the army's most dependable and hardest hitting, Winfield Scott Hancock. Even his men called him "Hancock the Superb."

The Pennsylvanian had amassed an enviable record as a combat leader. As a brigade commander with the VI Corps on the Peninsula in 1862, Hancock had shown real mettle, eventually earning him, in the days following Antietam, command of a II Corps division. He led the division with determination against Marye's Heights at Fredericksburg and later fought a brilliant two-front battle at Chancellorsville. In June 1863, he was given command of the entire corps, and just a few weeks later, at Gettysburg, he proved why he'd deserved the promotion. Hancock showed an eye for terrain and demonstrated the mind of a master tactician. Though wounded in that battle, Hancock recovered well enough to rejoin the army for the spring campaign of 1864.

In the Wilderness, Hancock held the vital Brock Road/Plank Road intersection. When he launched an offensive on the morning of May 6, he nearly drove Lee's entire right wing from the field, stopped only by the timely appearance of Longstreet's First Corps. Although held in reserve during the opening stages of Spotsylvania, and dangled as bait on May 9 and 10, Hancock performed well. Grant now planned something bigger for Hancock's 20,000 officers and men.

He looked to hit Lee square on the nose.

* * *

Although the II Corps occupied the extreme right of the army's position, Grant planned to shift them to the army's left-center, opposite the apex of the Mule Shoe Salient. Mott's bedraggled division, battered by the previous day's mis-timed debacle, would rejoin them. The corps would form up on the John C. Brown farm, where a woodlot would allow the men to get into position under protective cover. Then, just before dawn, they would advance to the tip of the salient and punch its way in, much the same way Upton's column had punched its way into Doles' Salient. The corps would then widen the breach, making room for Horatio Wright's entire VI Corps to stream into the gap.

To the east, Ambrose Burnside would attack in an effort to hold potential Confederate reinforcements in place. To the west, at Laurel Hill, Warren would likewise attack, although Grant expected him to support Hancock

IF UPTON COULD BREAK THROUGH WITH 4,500 MEN, WHAT COULD GRANT ACHIEVE WITH AN ENTIRE CORPS?

II Corps commander
Maj. Gen. Winfield
Scott Hancock (seated),
surrounded by three of his
division commanders
(from left), brigadier generals
Francis Barlow, David Bell
Birney, and John Gibbon.

and Wright with troops as needed.

Hancock's four divisions were commanded by an eclectic cadre of men. His most able division commander was Brig. Gen. John Gibbon. Although born in Pennsylvania, Gibbon had grown up in North Carolina, and at the battle of Fredericksburg his men fought a Confederate brigade in which three of his brothers served. A West Point graduate and artillery expert, he at one time commanded the famed "Black Hat Brigade," which later became the Iron Brigade because, at the battle of South Mountain, they "fought like iron." Gibbon had commanded his II Corps division since Chancellorsville.

Brigadier General David Bell Birney was a Pennsylvanian, as well, but not a trained soldier. He came from a family of Philadelphia abolitionists with deep political ties. After the outbreak of the war, he commanded the 23rd Pennsylvania Infantry, then moved steadily up the ranks, rising to temporary command of III Corps. Although not a favorite of Meade's, Birney had amassed a respectable fighting record.

Brigadier General Francis Barlow was a baby-faced New Yorker and Harvard-trained lawyer. Brave to a fault Barlow, like Birney, had no military training. He was attached to the 12th New York Infantry and then the

Hancock's division commanders: (from left) Barlow, Birney, and Gibbon; (below) Maj. Gen. Gershom Mott

61st New York Infantry earlier in the war, but he, too, rose steadily through the ranks and, at Gettysburg, found himself at the head of an XI Corps division. The men of the corps loathed him, though, and following his wounding on July 1, 1863, only two men in the entire division attempted to carry their commander from the field: one was shot in the act, and the other dropped him and made for the rear. Barlow nonetheless returned to the army and was given command of Hancock's old division in II Corps.

Hancock's final division commander was Gershom Mott, a Garden State native who'd proven a mixed bag as a commander. Although not trained as a soldier, he earned some experience leading men into combat during the Mexican War. During the Civil War, Mott served with the 5th and 6th New Jersey Infantry regiments and was wounded at Second Bull Run and Chancellorsville. His newly created, undersized division performed poorly in the Wilderness, however, and again on May 10. Like all of Hancock's division commanders, Mott was brave—but he was also in over his head.

Hancock briefed his commanders on the parameters of the plan but kept specific details secret. "We were told that it was a movement of more than usual importance," Barlow later said. "No information, so far as I can remember, was given to us as to the position or strength of the enemy, or as to the troops to be engaged in the movement . . . or as to the plan of the attack, or why any attack was to be made at that time or place."

*　*　*

As Hancock's division commanders did what they could to prepare with what information they had, Grant turned his attention back to Lee. Worried that the Confederate commander might slip away or even launch an attack of his own, Grant decided to pin him in place with a "reconnaissance in force" by Burnside.

As Burnside began to shift his troops around, and Hancock began to shift his troops around, too, word made it back to Confederate headquarters that something was up. Trying to make sense of the reports, Lee concluded that Grant was preparing to withdraw toward Fredericksburg. After all, when the armies had reached stalemate in the Wilderness, Grant had slipped around the Confederate left and continued to move on Richmond. In Spotsylvania, the armies had once more reached stalemate, so might not Grant again be trying to slip around the army?

Lee not only wanted to counter the Federal movement but, if possible, strike it as it marched. He ordered units to the Court House crossroads where he could easily launch them against a vulnerable Federal column. Because the artillery pieces at the tip of the Mule Shoe would have the farthest to travel, and they would have to do so over poorly maintained farm paths, Lee ordered them to withdraw first. They began to pull out in the late afternoon. Of the 30 guns that had been along the line, only four remained.

No one had bothered to tell Dick Ewell about the withdrawal, though. When Ewell had argued in favor of the Mule Shoe, he predicated his entire decision on having artillery. Without it, he knew the salient would be nearly impossible to hold—and now he found himself without the very artillery he needed to defend the position.

Nor had anyone told Ewell's division commander, Maj. Gen. Edward "Allegheny" Johnson, whose men occupied the salient's tip. Johnson only found out when one of his brigade commanders, Brig. Gen. George "Maryland" Steuart, sent him a panicked note. "The artillery along our front has been withdrawn," Steuart wrote, "by whose orders I know not and I beg that it be sent back immediately."

At age 48, Johnson was wily enough that Lee had

Farm roads like this one made it tough for Lee to maneuver his artillery quickly, despite his interior lines.

Maj. Gen. Edward "Allegheny" Johnson

Brig. Gen. George "Maryland" Steuart

considered him for promotion to corps command. It helped, too, that Johnson was a Virginia native—something Lee seemed to favor—although Johnson's family had moved to Kentucky while he was young and during childhood he attended school in Ohio. Johnson earned appointment to West Point, and during his subsequent army career, he developed a mischievous friendship with Winfield Scott Hancock. The two teamed up to play pranks on many of their fellow officers, making a formidable duo when unleashing their shenanigans on unsuspecting prey.

Johnson served in the United States army until 1861 when, three days before the firing on Fort Sumter, he resigned his commission—which led to his arrest. Held in Federal custody for a time, he traveled to Richmond on his release and was given command of the 12th Georgia Infantry. He spent the rest of 1861 serving in the western reaches of the Shenandoah Valley and was promoted to brigadier general in December of that year. When he heard news of the promotion, he was atop Allegheny Mountain—thus the nickname "Old Allegheny." Johnson later earned another nickname, "Old Clubby," because of his penchant for carrying a large walking stick in battle and whacking his men atop the head or back when he caught them not doing their full duty.

When Johnson got word from Steuart about the missing artillery, he sent word to Ewell. Ewell then appealed to Lee, twice, before the army commander finally acquiesced. It would take hours for the guns to start their way back to the line, though.

Even without the artillery, the works represented impressive engineering. "Trees were felled and piled upon each other, and a ditch dug behind them with the earth out of it thrown against the logs," said Brig. Gen. James Walker of the Stonewall Brigade, whose men were posted on the west side of the line midway between Doles' Salient and the tip of the Mule Shoe. "The limbs and tops of the trees as cut off from the trunks were used to form abattis, by placing them in front of the breastworks with the sharpened points toward the enemy."

Every 40 to 50 yards, soldiers built works perpendicular to the main line, an innovation known as a traverse. Traverses gave defenders something to pull back and duck behind in case of an enemy breakthrough, allowing the defender to seal the gap like watertight doors in a ship. Soldiers called them "hog pens."

Finally, incomplete segments of a second line, intended as a reserve line, ran about 50 yards behind the main line. Intended as a fallback position, Confederates never quite got around to finishing it.

Confederate earthworks posed
a formidable challenge.

As day wore into evening into night, the men posted along the Confederate line could hear noises off in the distance woods. They feared the worst, but Lee remained convinced it was the sound of a Federal withdrawal. Allegheny Johnson prowled the length of his line, urging his soldiers "to be on the alert" and ordering "some brigades to be awake all night, and all to be up in the trenches an hour or so before daylight." Crusty "Old Allegheny" expected the worst.

At the Bloody Angle

The Bloody Angle offers one of the most pristine experiences of any battlefield. What visitors see when they arrive is very similar to what the soldiers saw as they filed into positions here on May 8 and 9. The Park Service has installed interpretive markers that explain some of the action that took place in the field. A walking path made from recycled tires, shredded to look like bark, cuts a path through the tall grass. The butterflies and the deer come with the landscape.

Of course, the monument to the 126th Ohio (part of the Union VI Corps) didn't stand out in the field. That wasn't erected until May 15, 1914, after an appropriation from the state of Ohio. The regiment lost 70 men in its assaults against the Bloody Angle; the monument marks their farthest advance.

Near the parking lot, the forest juts out into the field

The monument to the 126th Ohio at the Bloody Angle

farther now than it did in 1864. As a result, the trees hide a monument that once stood in an open field. It's now tucked away in the woods to the right of the old farm lane, about 150 paces down from the gate. The monument is also hard to distinguish because of its design: a bronze plaque inset into a rock, sitting on a concrete base that looks much like a tree stump. The monument commemorates the work of Edward Stuart, whose father, George, did much to preserve the core area around the Bloody Angle. The younger Stuart continued that work.

The monument to Edward Stuart looks like a concrete tree stump in the woods. The monument's plaque reads: "Student of history, patriotic citizen and loyal companion whose interest and donations of land contributed largely to the establishment of the battlefield park."

Burnside Drive

Landrum House site

B

East Angle

A

D

E

Gordon Drive

F

C

I

Bloody Angle

The Muleshoe

McCoull House site

Stuart Monument

Ramseur Brigade Monument

H

Lee's Last Line

Grant Drive

Upton Monument

Doles' Salient

Confederate earthworks

G

Harrison House site

Anderson Drive

Union earthworks

Trails

Reconstructed Earthwork

Brock Road

613

Grant Drive

Exhibit Shelter

Sedgwick Monument

Hancock Road

Spindle Field

Block House Road

648

Maryland Brigade Monument

Laurel Hill

Brock Road

613

Walking Tour

| feet | 1000 |
0 .... Hal Jespersen

★ Driving Tour Stop 6
A Landrum Lane/Brown House Site
B Landrum House Site
C East Angle
D Johnson Captured
E End of Union Breakthrough
F Artillery Position
G "Lee to the Rear"
H McCoull House Site
I Bloody Angle

WALKING TOUR

While the Park Service's rubberized walking paths at the Bloody Angle provide an adequate overview of the action there, visitors can get a more comprehensive understanding of the battle by walking out Landrum Lane and then following the route of the attacking Federals into the Mule Shoe and along its eastern face, and then following the route of some of the Confederate counterattacks back out from the interior. The extended walk can take an hour and a half to two hours. Interpretation for sites A-F can be found in Chapter 8, for sites G and H in Chapter 9, and for site I in Chapter 10.

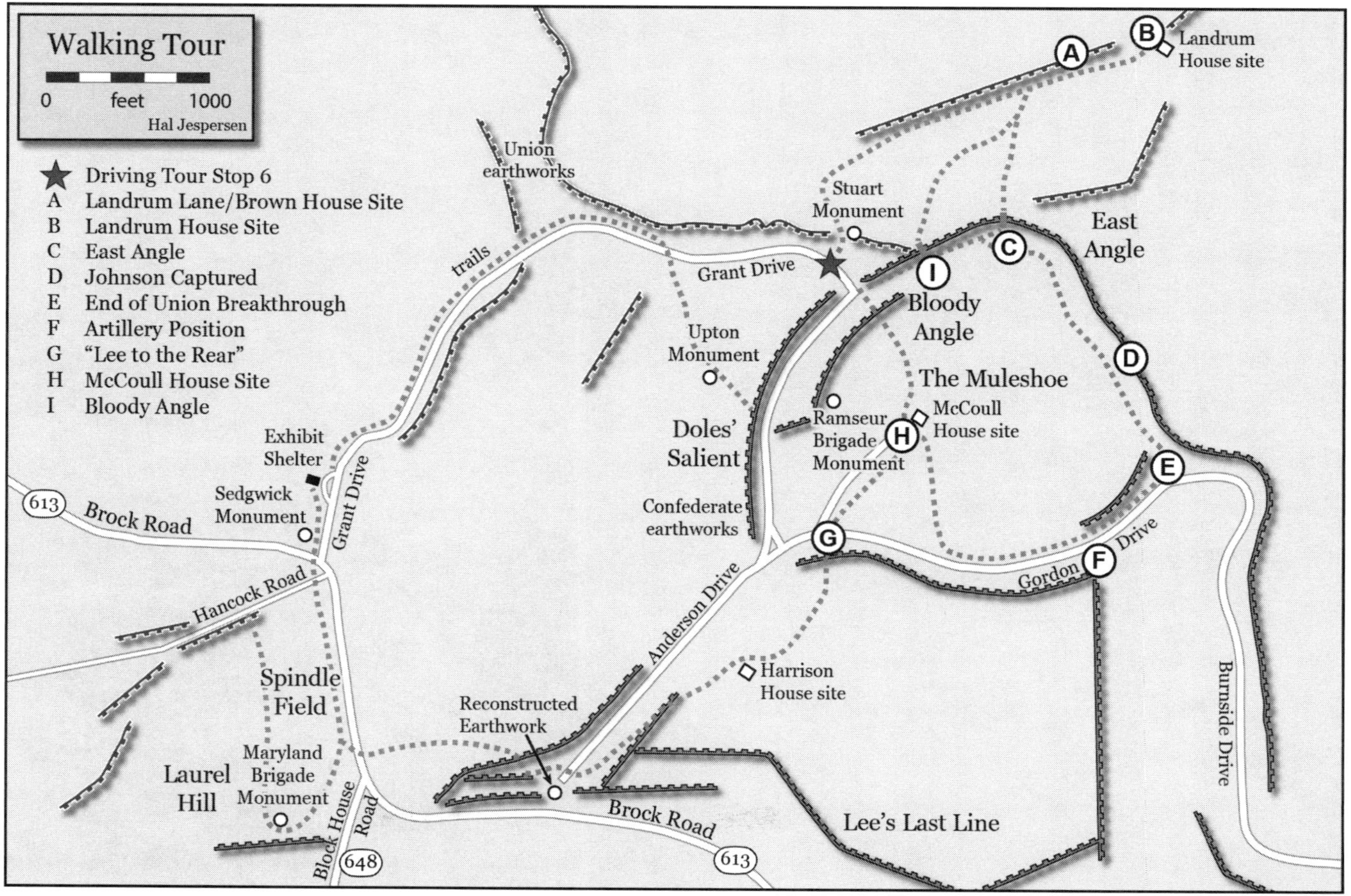

65

The Mule Shoe—Part I
The Union Attack

CHAPTER EIGHT

MAY 12, 1864—EARLY MORNING

The grueling heat that had been building since the armies first clashed in the Wilderness finally gave way in the late afternoon of May 11 to a rainstorm that drenched the armies and chilled them. "A cold, cheerless rain, falling in torrents," a Pennsylvanian grumbled. "The wind was raw and sharp, our clothes wet and we were just about as  disconsolate and miserable a set of men as ever were seen."

At 9:00 p.m., orders came down from Hancock for the men to pack up and hit the road. "Nobody knew where were going, but a rumor was started that we were going back to the rear to rest and wash our clothes," the Pennsylvania infantryman continued. "And this proved partially true, as it rained so hard all night that our clothes were thoroughly washed, but they needed wringing badly; I think I can safely say that of all our many night marches this one took the cake."

"[T]he roads were simply awful," one of Hancock's officers groaned, "rained continuously and mud was almost knee deep in places." Streams turned into raging rivers, and roads that had been dry and dusty turned into quagmires that sucked the men's shoes off with each step. "Every man followed his file leader, not by sight or touch, but by hearing him growl and swears, as he slipped, splashed and tried to pull his feet out of the mud," the Pennsylvanian added.

Literally and figuratively it was, in the words of another Union officer, "an intensely dark night."

"For heaven's sake," complained Federal division commander Francis Barlow, with at least some good humor, "at least face us in the right direction, so that we shall not march away from the enemy and have to round the world

A statue of a New Jersey soldier stands vigil over the Bloody Angle (inset and left)

Federal Assaults
May 12, 1864

miles

Hal Jespersen

Grant understood that Upton's attack on May 10 failed for want of support, so he decided to repeat the attack on a larger scale with more men and with ready reinforcements. On May 12, Hancock's II Corps would hammer the tip of the Mule Shoe, with Wright's VI Corps on hand to exploit the breakthrough. On the flanks, Warren's V Corps and Burnside's IX Corps would also launch attacks to tie down any potential Confederate reinforcements. Downpours and darkness delayed the main attack, and Warren's supporting attack got underway even hours later than that. Burnside launched on time but attacked with little vigor.

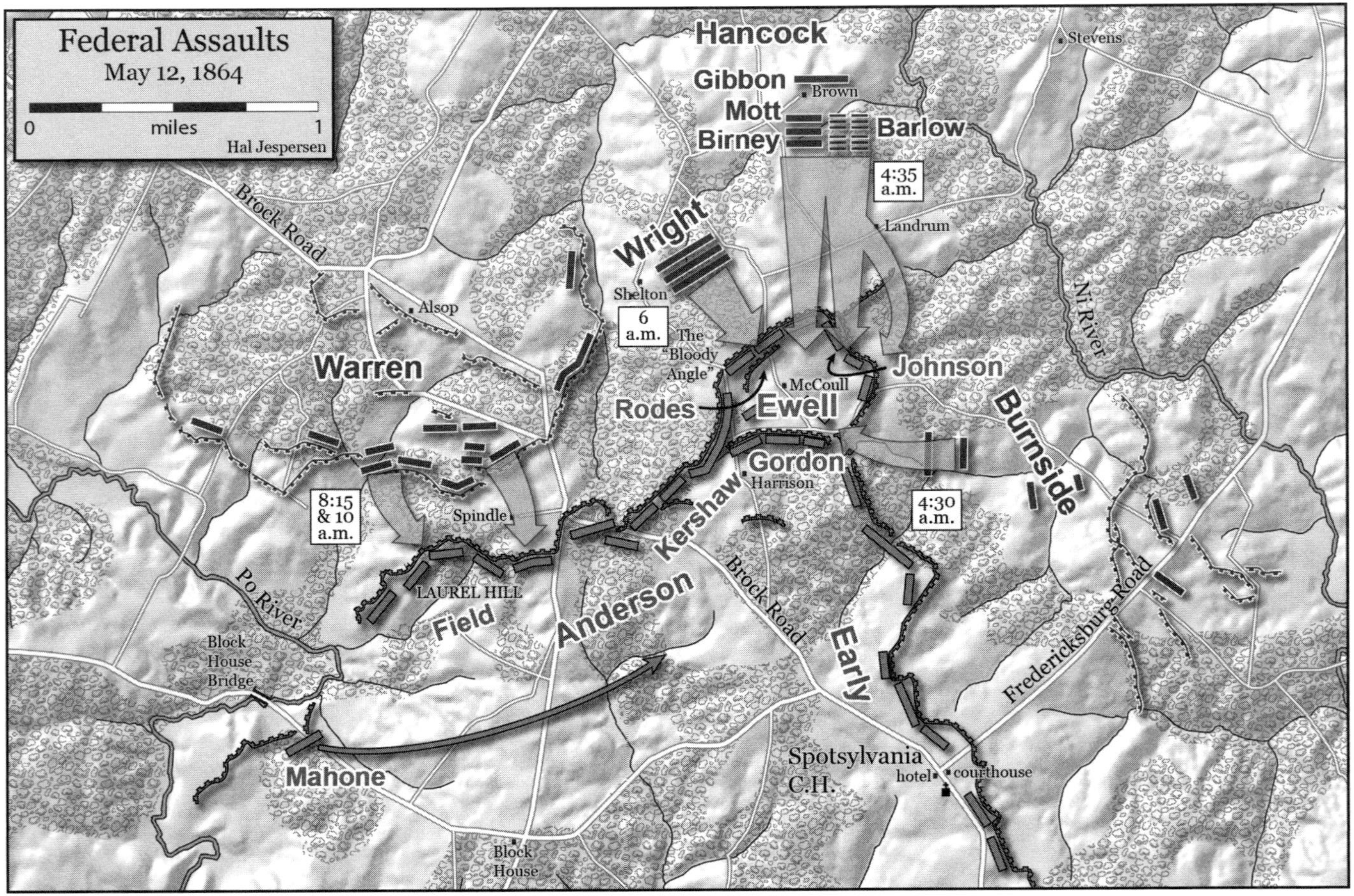

and come up in their rear."

By 3:00 a.m., even as the rain began to slacken, Hancock's men finally sloshed into place near the Brown farm. What torches lit their way, they extinguished so as not to give away their presence to any Confederate pickets.

"[W]e came to a halt in a low foggy pace, so chilly that our teeth chattered and our frames shook like leaves," said John Haley of the 17th Maine. "The mists of morning were very heavy and settled over us like a pall."

Some of the men dozed on their feet as they waited; others, knowing an attack was imminent, wrote final notes home. Officers shook hands and bade each other farewell. "Surrounded by the silence of night, by darkness and by fog, they stood, listening to raindrops as they fell from leaf to leaf," one of them remembered.

"There we stood in the drizzle," recalled the Mainer:

all orders given in whispers, and although we knew we faced a dreadful battle, we were not sorry to hear the voice of chanticleer, announcing the dawn of a new day. There was something terribly weird in this massing of troops at this time of day, in the hooting of owls as the dark figures of men moved through the pines, in the sobbing of the wind through the wet trees. The order to move to the attack wasn't half so disagreeable as one might think.

Four o'clock arrived—and passed. With fog now reducing visibility even further, Hancock worried about keeping his attack coordinated. He had aligned Barlow in a traditional line of battle with a wide front, but he had stacked Birney's men in a compact column similar to Upton's fist-like formation two days earlier, with Mott's men following immediately behind as support. Gibbon's men were held in reserve. Out front, the 1st and 2nd United States Sharpshooters and the 66th New York Infantry would advance as skirmishers.

As Hancock met with his commanders, a mule broke loose from one of Barlow's New York regiments. The

Alfred Waud sketched the view from the Brown house.

The II Corps attacks.

animal, which carried all the kitchen implements for the regiment, created such a racket that the men of the regiment ran it down and tackled it to the ground, holding it there until the assault column passed.

That order forward finally came at 4:35 a.m.

"And then," wrote one Federal,

in the dim gray light of that early spring morning, with a mist rising from the field and thicket, and while the birds were faintly chirping in the bushes and trees as they noted the coming of dawn, the grand old First Division moved forward in almost perfect silence.

Hancock, sitting on horseback, watched his men step off. "I know they will not come back!" he lamented. "They will not come back!"

*   *   *

As stealthily as possible, the blue host moved through the woods from the Brown farm toward the Confederate picket line posted along the sunken Landrum farm lane. "[O]n we went, a solid mass, moving very rapidly," wrote one of Barlow's staffers.

They burst out of the woods and swept so overwhelmingly into the farm lane that the Southern skirmishers never fired a shot. "[T]hey had to do one of two things, surrender or skip," said a New Yorker, "and I think every picket in front of our line skipped for dear life."

In their exuberance, many Federals "let forth a yell which woke people in Washington"—giving away their presence to Confederates across the valley. As the overwhelmed pickets turned tail and ran into the fog, the stunned Federals belatedly realized their error. "[T]he red earth of a well defined line of works loomed up through the mists on the crest of another ridge, distant about two hundred yards with

a shallow ravine between," one soldier reported.

So officers steadied their lines for the final push—and across the field they charged.

Federals swarm over the crest of the Confederate works.

* * *

Between the loud huzzah from across the field and the scared pickets that began leaping into the trenches, Confederates had plenty of warning about the oncoming attack. Most had been awake all night, either manning the works or keeping warm around their campfires, their rifles stacked and ready. Anyone on the line could see, even through the fog, the landscape out front grow dark as the Federal soldiers swept over it. "They came in seventeen lines, one line behind the other; and we counted them," wrote Thomas Reed of the 7th Louisiana. "[S]ome fellow said: 'Look out, boys! We will have blood for supper!'"

"Well," Reed continued, "before suppertime we had lots of blood."

Union soldiers knew they'd been spotted. "We see the frowning earth-works in our front lined with the now thoroughly aroused enemy, whose every eye was taking deadly aim over the long line of glittering muskets resting beneath the logs which crowned the rampart," one recalled.

"The moment for the Confederate line had come," realized Confederate Brig. Gen. James Walker. Walker, known as "Stonewall Jim" because he commanded the famed Stonewall Brigade, ordered his men to take up their stacked arms and prepared to deliver a withering volley. His men steadied themselves, took aim, waited . . .

"Fire!" Walker roared—but the rifles of his men only went Pop! Pop! Pop! not Bang! Bang! Bang! The

Brig. Gen. James "Stonewall Jim" Walker

Lee rushed his artillery back into position over muddy roads—but the move came too late. Some arrived on the scene just in time to get captured.

butternuts had loaded their weapons the night before. Stacked as they'd been, with their muzzles up, the torrential rain overnight had leaked down the barrels and wet the gunpowder. When the hammers fell upon the percussion caps, the caps went off but the guns would not discharge.

The Federals hit the abatis—which might have posed a serious obstacle in the face of any close-quarters rifle fire—and then suddenly they were into the Confederate line. "The mad mass surges on over the entrenchments, in a restless terrible wave which sweeps all before it," said one soldier.

Colonel William Witcher's all-Virginia brigade was the first to be hit. A small hillock in front of his line had split the attack column in two, and the Federals came over at two points. Men of the 26th Michigan and 140th Pennsylvania—two of Barlow's regiments—vaulted over the works at the salient's tip and along its northeastern face.

"The bayonet was freely used on both sides, the enemy fought desperately, and nothing but the formation of our attack and the desperate valor of our troops could have carried the point," said Col. John R. Brooke.

Within moments, Witcher's brigade nearly ceased to exist. George Steuart's brigade fell next. He and the bulk of his Tar Heels and Virginians were captured and sent to the rear.

Old Allegheny, who'd slept in his clothes, "ready to leap to a horse in a moment's notice," rushed to the battle line. According to one witness, Johnson mounted the earthworks, smacking men over the head with his club with one hand and batting away Yankee bayonets with the other until the Federal swarm finally swallowed him.

Along the northwest side of the salient, the Federal storm overwhelmed the famed Louisiana Brigade. "I have as you know been in a good many hard fights, but I never saw anything like the contest of the 12th," stated one of the Tigers.

"Every Confederate realized the desperate situation

and every Union soldier knew what was involved," said a Maine man. "For a time, every soldier was a fiend. The attack was fierce—the resistance fanatical."

It was, he said, "a tempest of iron and lead . . . a rain of fire."

Beyond the Louisianans, "Stonewall Jim" Walker did what he could to rally his Stonewall Brigade. Some of his men tried to clear their fouled weapons, while others simply used them as clubs and spears. "Then ensued one of those hand-to-hand encounters with clubbed rifles, bayonets, swords, and pistols which defies description," recalled one New York officer.

Walker went down with a bullet in the arm. His men crumbled around him. "On the 12th of May, 1864," Walker later mourned, "the famous Stonewall Brigade ceased to exist."

Into the fray—finally—rolled Lee's absent artillery. Although a few guns managed to fire off a round or two before being overrun, most of the guns never had the chance to even unlimber; the blue wave swept over them even as they rolled into position. Some artillerists attempted to turn around and flee with their guns, but innovative Yankees simply shot the horses.

*   *   *

In 30 minutes, Hancock's corps ripped open a hole in the Confederate line nearly half a mile wide and half a mile deep. Of the 4,500 men in Johnson's division, the II Corps took 3,000 of them prisoner—including "Maryland" Steuart and "Allegheny" Johnson. Hancock also captured 30 stands of colors and 20 cannon (two more would be taken by the corps the next morning).

But even as word went up the chain of command to Meade and Grant about Hancock's victory, the II Corps' momentum finally fizzled. Along the eastern face of the Mule Shoe, stout resistance from Brig. Gen. James Lane's North Carolinians—already beleaguered by bumbling pressure from Ambrose Burnside—managed to stem the blue tide. "The honor and the safety of the army demand it," Lane said.

Along the western face of the Mule Shoe, Brig. Gen. Junius Daniels's men stemmed the tide there, although Daniels himself was shot in the bowels and would die the next day.

In the interior of the Mule Shoe, Federals made it just past the high ground of the McCoull farm. "We followed up the enemy driving them before us through the woods and brush up to another interior line of entrenchments occupied by another line of troops," said a New Jerseyman. By that point, Federals had "no regimental or company

"EVERY CONFEDERATE REALIZED THE DESPERATE SITUATION AND EVERY UNION SOLDIER KNEW WHAT WAS INVOLVED. FOR A TIME, EVERY SOLDIER WAS A FIEND."

organizations left, but a disorganized and shattered line devoid of organization," an officer said.

A soldier from Maine summed it up best: "The force of the blow was spent."

Now it was the Confederates' turn.

Tracing the Federal Attack

STOP A: The original road trace of Landrum Lane, sunken into the ground, runs parallel to the modern footpath on the northernmost edge of the fields that front the Mule Shoe. Confederates posted their pickets along this line, which they then fortified by throwing up more dirt

on the lane's north side. The Civilian Conservation Corps further "enhanced" the earthworks in the 1930s.

A hiker walking back along Landrum Lane will notice how the road actually runs diagonally away from the Mule Shoe. From the Landrum house, the distance from the lane to the Confederate line is more than twice as far as it was back at the west end of the lane. When Hancock's men pounced on the Confederate pickets, they reformed along the road before resuming their attack. The soldiers closest

The modern Landrum Lane (in photo, right) runs parallel to the historic road bed (in photo, center), which is sunken; the Confederate pickets fortified the roadbed with a line of works (in photo, left). All three features are easily visible on a walk to the Landrum house site.

to the Landrum house had farther to go. They ended up wheeling to the southwest in order to keep up with their counterparts at the west end of the lane. Partway across the field, a hillock forced them to wheel around even farther, so they ended up hitting the eastern face of the salient and not directly at its tip.

Partway down the road, a pair of NPS historical markers offers a good reference point for the Brown farm, which stood about one-half mile farther to the north through the forest, and no longer stands. Hancock assembled his attack force on the fields of the Brown farm and then advanced in this direction.

Once Hancock's men had broken through the salient, II Corps artillerists set up some 30 guns along Landrum Lane and began to pound Confederate positions, many at nearly point blank range.

STOP B: Winfield Scott Hancock made his headquarters in the home that sat here, owned by Willis and Lucy Landrum (see Appendix B). He eventually vacated after the house came under intense counterbattery fire from the Confederates shooting at the artillery pieces Hancock had placed on the property. The house was destroyed in the battle. The ruins of the home's two fireplaces remain to mark its location.

A thick table of a monument, topped by a bronze plaque, also squats in the Landrum clearing. Dedicated in May 1940 by the Military Order of the Loyal Legion of the United States (MOLLUS), the monument recognizes the group's efforts to preserve the landscape. MOLLUS was one of several military societies established after the war "to commemorate the events and principles of the War for the Union." Such societies, North and South, did much to shape American memory about the war.

Remains of the Landrum house's two chimneys—one at either end of the house—mark the home's original location.

Walking back toward the western end of the lane, hikers can clearly see the undulations in the field that affected the movement of Hancock's men during their initial attack. Later, those undulations would offer protection to Federal soldiers from Confederate counterattacks.

A "Y" in the path leads down into a gulley. At the bottom, it's easy to see the funnel-shaped swale that directed Federal reinforcements westward toward the Bloody Angle. The low ground offers shelter from Confederates firing from the earthworks above.

STOP C: The area at the tip of the Mule Shoe is known today as the East Angle. Although it's at the apex of the salient, this bend in the line has always been defined by its position relative to the more notorious Bloody Angle, which sits farther west.

At about 4:50 a.m. on the rainy morning of May 12, the 26th Michigan punched the Confederate position squarely on the nose. A little to the east, the 140th Pennsylvania swept over the works at nearly the same time. A hiker standing on the footbridge can look to the right and see where Maj. Gen. David Birney's division broke through and swept along the Confederate line, held here by Louisiana troops and the Stonewall Brigade; to the left, the rest of Barlow's division swept

Although a cannon now sits at the tip of the Mule Shoe, Lee had pulled his artillery out on May 11.

into the lines, sweeping up a Virginia brigade under William Witcher.

Confederate Capt. William Carter's artillery pieces—among those ordered away by Lee and then later ordered to return—rolled back into position here near the footbridge even as Federals flooded in. Carter got off one round before being overrun. "Don't shoot my men!" he cried.

"Maryland" Steuart and "Allegheny" Johnson as prisoners

This small board was the makeshift monument to the site of Allegheny Johnson's capture. It eventually fell victim to the elements.

STOP D: As Allegheny Johnson stood atop these earthworks, swinging his hickory walking stick at invading Federals, it's hard to believe no one shot him down. Instead, Federals took him captive. After the war a simple wooden sign was mounted atop the work marking the spot of the generals capture, unfortunately the sign was lost to time and nature. Sent to the rear, Johnson found himself at the headquarters of his old friend, Hancock. "General Johnson, I am glad to see you," Hancock said warmly.

"This is damned bad luck," Johnson groaned, "yet I would have had this good fortune fall to you than to any other living man." Witnesses later saw Johnson sitting on a stack of ammunition boxes, head in hands, weeping.

Johnson's subordinate, Brig. Gen. George "Maryland" Steuart, was not so magnanimous in defeat. He was captured in the same area. When asked for his officer's sword by his captor, he barked, "Sir, you all waked us up so early this morning that I didn't have time to get it on." When brought before Hancock, Steuart shot daggers from his eyes. Hancock nonetheless offered his hand. Steuart rebuffed it. "Under existing circumstances, Sir, I cannot take your hand," he growled.

"And under any other circumstances, I should not have offered it," Hancock said, withdrawing the offered hand. The corps commander sent both generals to the rear with the other prisoners. As a courtesy to his friend, he gave Johnson a horse to ride; he made Steuart walk.

STOP E: Brigadier General James Lane fought a two-front battle on May 12. To the west, the bumbling Burnside tied down the North Carolinian's men; from the north, Barlow's men came sweeping down. Thankfully, chaos, exhaustion, unclear orders, and topography all conspired to rob Federals of their momentum. For instance, a deep fishbowl in the landscape behind the Confederate line here threw Federals into confusion, directing them toward the interior of the Mule Shoe instead of farther along the earthworks. Lane's men held firm at this spot, stemming the Federal advance.

That was especially fortuitous for Confederates, who actually had a 100-yard gap in the line that started on this crest and dropped steeply into a stream-cut ravine before rising to a small plateau (Stop F, next). The terrain—steep-sided and wet at the bottom—would have been difficult to man, but with command of the high ground on either side, plus its tucked-away location relative to the rest of the line, Lee had not expressed worry about its defensibility.

A giant punchbowl in the terrain served to funnel Federal troops into the interior of the Mule Shoe, blunting their momentum and relieving pressure on Lane's beleagured troops.

STOP F: As part of his efforts to bottle up both Burnside and Barlow, Lane deployed artillery on a small plateau that overlooked the gap in the Confederate line. Here, the Confederate line that had bulged out at the salient resumed its otherwise smooth east-to-west curve.

Remains of the earthworks still cross the table-flat parcel. From the plateau, the earthworks run westward parallel to Gordon Drive. Brigadier General John Brown Gordon's men constructed the works as a fallback position prior to the Federal breakthrough on May 12, but they served as a useful rallying point for fleeing Confederates.

The remains of Gordon's reserve line look like giant-carved grooves in the ground.

⟶ TO STOP 6

From the Bloody Angle, continue along Grant Drive 0.2 miles. You will see a dirt pull off on the right, where you can stop to look around if you wish. This marks the location of Upton's breakthrough on May 10. The path from the woods will be clearly visible.

Continue along Grant Drive 0.2 miles to the Y-intersection and bear left onto Gordon Drive. Follow Gordon Drive for 400 feet and turn left onto McCoull House Lane and follow it to its terminus 0.2 miles ahead.

GPS: N 38.22021 W 77.59974

The Mule Shoe—Part II
The Confederate Counterattacks

CHAPTER NINE
MAY 12, 1864—MORNING

It was the silence that bothered John Brown Gordon.

The Confederate brigadier knew something was amiss. Positioned in a reserve line near the base of the Mule Shoe, he had received a note saying "there's something wrong down there in the woods where General Johnson's men are"—but through the forest and fog, he could neither see nor hear a thing. "There was little or no shooting in the front line to indicate any fighting," wrote one of Gordon's men, "and this alone informed us of the disaster."

Thin, with a high peaked forehead and a bushy goatee, the 38-year-old Gordon embodied the ideal citizen soldier. A lawyer before the war, he had signed up with a company of irregular mountaineers, "The Raccoon Roughs," and the men elected him captain. From there, he earned the command of the 6th Alabama, and then worked the rest of his way up the ranks by putting himself in the thick of some of the hardest fighting of the war. At Malvern Hill, he was wounded in the eye—an injury that ever-after gave him a hangdog but determine look.

It had been at Antietam that September where Gordon really learned to know chaos. Charged with holding a sunken road at the center of the Southern position, Gordon's men staved off waves of Union attacks. Gordon

Maj. Gen. John Brown Gordon (inset)

The final Confederate counter-attacks had to push their way up this slope even as a swale in front of the works funneled Federals to this very same spot. Trenches once deep enough to stand in have eroded over time to look like little more than dips and humps.

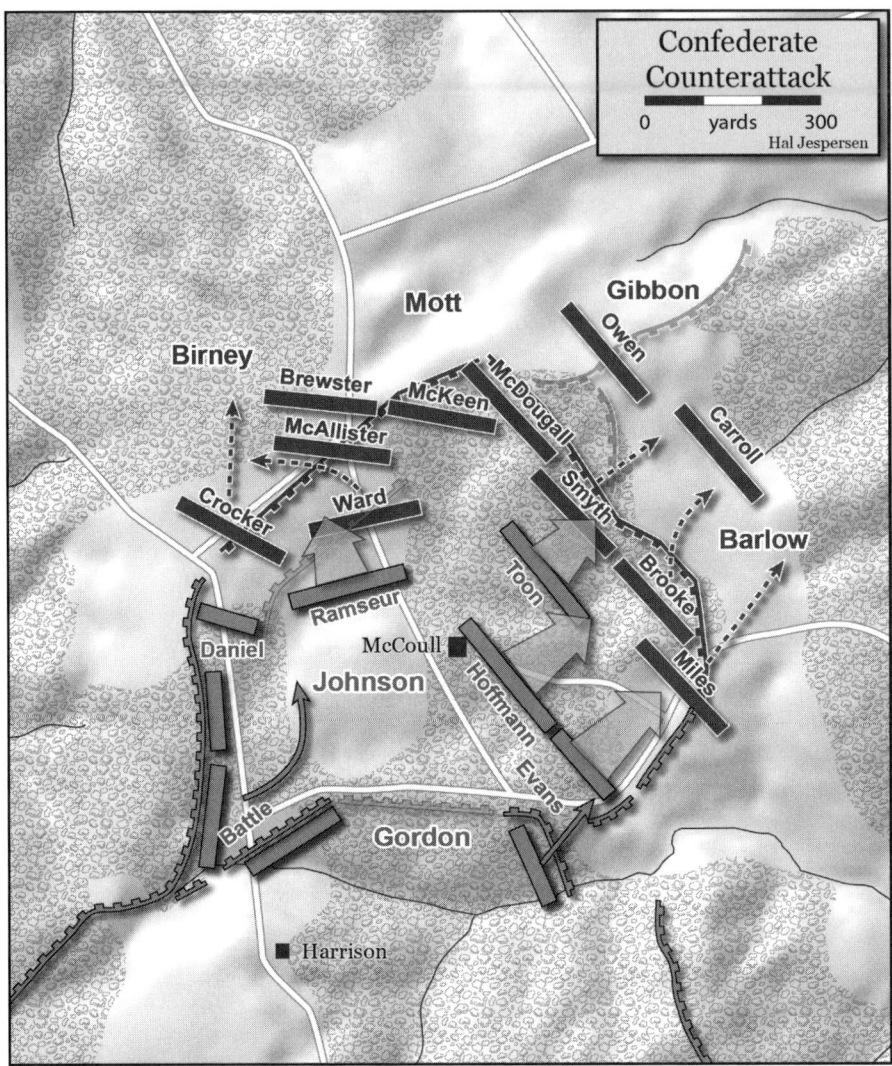

Confederate Counterattack

0   yards   300

Hal Jespersen

Mott

Gibbon

Owen

Birney

Brewster

McKeen

McDougall

McAllister

Carroll

Crocker

Ward

Smyth

Barlow

Toon

Brooke

Ramseur

McCoull

Daniel

Johnson

Hoffmann

Miles

Evans

Battle

Gordon

Harrison

CONFEDERATE COUNTERATTACK

Because of the uncoordinated attacks elsewhere along the Federal line, Lee had the ability to shift reinforcements into place for counterattacks against the II Corps. As they began streaming onto the battlefield, infantry from the Federal VI Corps also began pushing onto the field from the opposite direction, ultimately converging on the same spot along the northwest face of the salient.

prowled back and forth along his line, taking bullets in his leg, his left arm, his shoulder. The bullet that finally stopped him passed through his cheek and out his jaw, and he collapsed face-first into his hat. He would have drowned in his own blood had it not drained out a bullet hole.

He was back for the next invasion of the North, however, leading a Second Corps brigade in Jubal Early's division. Gordon's men made it all the way to the banks of the Susquehanna River—the furthest advance of any of Lee's men. On orders, they pulled back toward Gettysburg just in time to help rout the Union XI Corps north of town. As Gordon told it, he offered succor to a wounded Federal officer whom he found on a small knoll—Francis Barlow, abandoned by the XI Corps men who loathed him so much.

Most recently in the Wilderness, Gordon led a late-day

attack against the Union right flank—an attack that might have achieved more had darkness not halted it. Gordon had petitioned for an earlier start time, but Early had dithered, and the unsatisfactory result left bad feelings between them. Early's temporary promotion to Thirds Corps command, and Gordon's promotion to fill Early's position at the division level, diffused the situation for the moment.

Lee considered Gordon one of his best officers, "characterized by splendid audacity"—high praise indeed from an army commander whose middle name, it was said, was "audacity itself."

As Gordon peered into the silent fog, shapes began to materialize: refugees fleeing from the collapsing front line. To buy time, Gordon quickly threw Brig. Gen. Robert Johnston's brigade forward while he organized a stronger defense. As the Georgian pulled together two more brigades, Lee appeared out of the thinning mist, riding his gray horse, Traveller. "Not a word did he say, but simply took off his hat, and as he sat on his charger I never saw a man look so noble, or a spectacle so impressive," a soldier later remembered.

Lee's expression, though, showed a hint of despair. He rode to the front of Gordon's formation as though to lead it into the breach, but Gordon grabbed Traveller's bridle. "These men have never failed! They never will!" Gordon cried, more to the men than to Lee. "Will you, boys?"

"No! No!" they cried back. "We will not fail!" And then a new cry broke out, one that had been heard on the

"Lee to the rear!"

Gordon's reserve line runs parallel to the park road along a path that roughly cuts off the base of the Mule Shoe.

morning of May 6 in the Wilderness when Lee tried to lead a brigade of Texans into the fight, and again on May 10 when Lee tried to plug the gap at Doles' Salient: "Lee to the rear! Lee to the rear!" The men knew their commander was far too valuable to go into combat, and they forced the commanding general back.

Then Gordon gave the command: "Charge!"

"All saw that a crisis was upon us," a soldier later wrote. "If we failed, the consequence would be disastrous to the extreme."

*   *   *

With Gordon leading reinforcements forward, Lee turned his attention to the larger situation. He knew he couldn't hold the salient, so he needed a fallback position. He directed Martin Luther Smith and his engineers to construct a new mile-long line across the base of the salient. With the survivors of Johnson's shattered division available as a labor force, Lee had the men he needed, but he desperately needed more time. To get that time, he chose to buy it with lives.

Had Grant's grand offensive unfolded as it should have, things might have turned out very differently. Burnside's feeble efforts against the eastern face of the Mule Shoe successfully tied down most of the Third Corps, but did little else. At the other end of the line, Warren remained inexplicably silent. The man who had been too eager to jump the gun two days earlier now dragged his feet—and would do so for four more hours—which gave Lee a free hand to draw reinforcements from that sector of his works.

As Lee began patching together other counterattacks, Gordon's men pushed through the interior of the salient toward its eastern face. "Onward they swept, pouring their rapid volleys into Hancock's confused ranks, and swelling the deafening din of battle with piercing shouts," the brigadier recalled. His brigades struck those of Nelson Miles, Thomas Smyth, and John R. Brooke, forcing the Federals back. "[The Confederates] seemed determined to gain back at any cost what had been lost, and the most severe close fighting of the war ensued," said a Union staff officer.

Gordon's men linked up with Lane's men, still mounting a stout resistance, and their combined effort recaptured the eastern face of the salient. Federals didn't retreat far, however; just outside the Confederate works, they constructed works of their own, just yards away, sometimes piling dead bodies atop one another for added protection.

On the western face of the salient, Brig. Gen. Cullen Battle drove his Alabamians into the fight like "a solid

wedge driven into the very heart of the enemy."

Brigadier General Stephen Ramseur then drove his North Carolinians into the fight. First, they had to capture an interior line of works, which they did without firing a shot. Using that position as a jumping-off point, they fixed bayonets and charged the Federals in the outer works—although they did so without their commander, who'd been wounded by an artillery shot.

"[The Yankees] cut down at least one third of our boys," recalled Ramseur's second in command, Col. Bryan Grimes. "[N]ot withstanding this withering fire our boys made no halt, other than to pour into the enemies ranks, if possible a more deadly fire, for as we drove them the land we charged over was literally covered with the enemies dead. The field was perfectly blue with them."

Once in the main works, Grimes turned his men toward the north and began recapturing more stretches of the works. "[W]e fought fearful odds," a North Carolinian said,

and it was here for the first time that I ever knew the enemy to run upon our bayonets, but they came down with such fury that we pitched many of them with the bayonet right over into the ditch. The water was so bloody in the ditches that one inexperienced would have taken it for blood entire, though the water was about one foot deep in the trenches where we fought.

As Ramseur's men left the reserve works, Brig. Gen.

Ramseur's brigade charged into the melee across the open fields of the McCoull farm. First they had to recapture an inner line of works, which can be seen about 50 yards to the left of the monument. Then they had to charge over a rise in the ground and into the heart of the storm.

Brig. Gen. Stephen D. Ramseur

Brig. Gen. Abner Perrin

Perrin's grave in Fredericksburg's Confederate Cemetery

The McCoull farm (below)

Abner Perrin's Alabama brigade rolled forward to take their position. Earlier, Perrin had said he would come out of the fight a live major general or a dead brigadier. As he mounted the reserve line of works to drive his men forward to the main line, Perrin was shot seven times. He left the field a dead brigadier and was later buried in Fredericksburg's City Cemetery.

"Our first charge was straight into the Angle," said one of Perrin's men, who charged through the yard of the McCoull farm:

As I passed under a large cherry tree near the front gate I distinctly remember the shower of the bits of leaves floating to the ground in the still sultry air. They were falling in a constant shower from the whole tree, and, as I passed through them, I remember that the sight at the moment suggested to my mind, a constant fall of snow falling to the ground with that easy quiet motion peculiar to it, when there is not a breath of wind. The enemy must have been overshooting us wonderfully, for, if the bullets had been sweeping close to the ground as thick as they were through that tree, I don't see how any of us could have gotten through.

Next, Brig. Gen. Nathaniel Harris brought his four Mississippi regiments to the fight. The Mississippians had been constructing earthworks earlier in the day, so some carried their rifles as well as small hatchets in their belts. When they fell upon the Federals, they used both their rifles and hatchets freely.

"The breastworks were slippery with blood and rain," one of them said, "dead bodies lying underneath half trampled out of sight."

One of the final brigades to come into action were the 1,300 South Carolinans of Brig. Gen. Samuel McGowan.

McGowan's men had been humiliated in Wilderness, driven from the line on May 6—in front of Robert E. Lee, no less. "My God! General McGowan, is this splendid brigade of yours running like a flock of geese?" Lee had bellowed.

"General, the men are not whipped," McGowan retorted. "They only want a place to form, and will fight as well as they ever did." And indeed they did, but the incident stuck with McGowan. Now he had redemption in mind. "[W]ith a cheer and at the double quick, plunging through mud knee deep," his men charged in. McGowan went down with a bullet in the right arm—his fourth wound of the war.

It was 9:00 a.m.

Brig. Gen. Samuel McGowen

With McGowan's strength added to the line, Confederates still did not have enough manpower to fight all the way back to the apex of the Mule Shoe. Instead, they made it about halfway up a gentle incline, 200 yards short. The topography gave Federals the advantage of high ground, but of more concern was the topography on the far side of the works. The open ground between Landrum Lane and the salient dipped into a shallow valley that cut diagonally across the field. As Federal reinforcements crossed, they found themselves in the ravine—and tended to stay in it as long as possible because of the protection it provided. As a result, they advanced up its length, which funneled them to the very spot where McGowan's men had advanced to.

Said one Confederate: "It was plainly a question of bravery and endurance now."

Tracing the Confederate Counterattacks

STOP G: For the third time in a week, Confederates faced annihilation. Grant had hammered the right flank of Lee's army on May 6 in the Wilderness, he had punched through Dole's Salient on May 10, and now he had split the Army of Northern Virginia in two and was widening the gap. Each time, Robert E. Lee responded as the model of courage, ready to lead his men into battle to save the army—and each time, his army held him back. As had happened the two times previously, soldiers surrounded their commander and cried, "Lee to the rear! Lee to the rear!"

From the Harrison house site, looking toward the McCoull house site. Lee rode along this route in response to the sound of battle.

Lee had been approaching the McCoull house from the Harrison house to the south. A footpath takes hikers in that direction through fields that turned into fields of slaughter

The remains of the Harrison house

on May 18. Over a trickle at the bottom of a ditch and back up again, the path leads to the Harrison house site (see Chapter 14). From there, it winds parallel to some of the most impressive works in the park.

Coming from the Harrison house, Lee reached the end of the McCoull farm lane when he encountered Gordon preparing to lead his men in a counterattack. Lee prepared to lead them himself when the familiar cry arose. Gordon convinced his commander that he would take care of business in the front, leaving Lee to attend to business constructing a new line farther to the rear.

STOP H: Neil McCoull owned a 600-acre farm that made up the heart of what became know as the Mule Shoe, growing mostly corn and grain, aside from the farmhouse he owned in a little knoll and which he shared with his three spinster sisters. The women were at home at the time of the battle, which raged around the house. The women made it through unhurt and the farmhouse ultimately survived, although it burncd down years later.

The foundation of the McCoull house

The May 12 firestorm across the property left the ground littered with corpses: some 14,500 Federals and uncounted Confederates. After the war, Confederates were reburied in the Confederate Cemetery in Spotsylvania Court House. Federals were reburied in the new National Cemetery at Fredericksburg.

To the west of the clearing, in almost a straight line with the spot where Emory Upton broke through on May 10, a granite slab stands in the middle of the field. Dedicated in the fall of 2001, the monument commemorates the action of Stephen Dodd Ramseur's brigade, which stormed across this section of the field to retake a double line of works captured during the Federal breakthrough on May 12. The innermost line of those works can be seen not far from the monument; a small hill separates them from the main Confederate line on the other side.

Ewell called Ramseur "the hero of the day" for leading his men into battle as he did. While they successfully retook the line, Ramseur fell injured and his brigade took as many as 50 percent casualties. "Deo vindice," the monument reads: "God will defend us."

To the east of the McCoull clearing, a Park Service road leads to a maintenance facility (which is not accessible by the public). The building is the last surviving structure from the Civilian Conservation Corps (C.C.C.) encampment that filled the entire clearing in the 1930s. The camp included five barracks that housed a couple hundred men; officers quarters; a repair shop; a blacksmith shop; a mess hall; a recreation building; and a half-dozen other smaller outbuildings, including latrines (See Appendix C).

The hillside today (below) was a cemetery for many of Harris' Mississippians (left).

To the north of the McCoull clearing, a footpath runs down to the McCoull spring. Although a blessing during the battle, and still in use by the C.C.C., the water is no longer potable.

From the capped spring, a look back at the face of the open hill side offers a look at an early Confederate cemetery. Following the battle, the Mississippians of Nathaniel Harris' brigade were interred here. Harris' men had charged into the fight at the Bloody Angle along a route that roughly matches the footpath through the woods.

→ TO THE BLOODY ANGLE

If following the walking tour, take the footpath through the woods to the Bloody Angle. Be aware of the uneven ground as you walk. If following the driving tour, either follow the footpath or skip ahead to chapter 10 and follow the directions at the end of the chapter.

The Mule Shoe—Part III
The Bloody Angle

CHAPTER TEN
MAY 12-13, 1864

"May God save me from another such scene," said Priv. Elisha Hunt Rhodes of the 2nd Rhode Island.

Confederates pushing up the slope along the western face of the Mule Shoe . . . Hancock's II Corps struggling against them to hold open the gap they'd created . . . Wright's VI Corps funneling up the ravine and swirling into the maelstrom . . . rain drenching . . . trenches flooding . . . soldiers fighting, bleeding, dying . . . .

"To advance was impossible, to retreat was death," said Union staff officer Robert Robertson. "The ground drank its fill of blood."

For 17 more hours, in pouring rain, in water and mud up to their shins, with guns and bayonets and hatchets and fists, soldiers grappled in the most prolonged intense hand-to-hand combat of the war. "Fresh troops from the other corps were continually being pushed up to the salient, in vain endeavors to make a new assault on the enemy's line within," Robertson said. "[T]he heaps of dead, the pools of blood, and the terrific volleys of musketry, were too much for man's endurance."

"All around that salient was a seething, bubbling, roaring hell of hate and murder," said John Haley of the 17th Maine.

Soldiers described it as "a panopoly of horror," "a pandemonium of terror," "a literal saturnalia of blood." One described it as "a Gologtha"—a place of skulls.

A shell lodged in a tree (inset)

"I have heard that blood-drenched bullet-swept angle, called 'Hell's Half-acre,'" Robertson added.

A close-up of the text from the monument of the 49th New York Infantry at the Bloody Angle.

Many called it "the slaughter-pen of Spottsylvania." Most remembered it as the Bloody Angle.

"At every assault and every repulse, new bodies fell

Men used rifles as clubs. Others fired at point-blank range. The bayonet was employed freely.

upon the heaps of the slain, and over the filled ditches they fought on the corpses of the fallen," said a New Jersey officer. "The wounded were covered by the killed, and expired under piles of their comrades' bodies."

With the lines only feet apart, combatants fired at each other at point-blank range. "Sometimes they would grab one of our guns and wrench it from us," recalled a New Yorker, who took several Confederate guns the same way.

One Vermonter on the front line remembered "nothing but a breastwork of logs between us and the enemy, where we would stab over with our bayonets[.] [M]en would jump up on the works and his comrades would hand him our muskets and he would stand there and fire until shot down when another would take his place and so continue."

"The bullets sang like swarming bees, and their sting was death," Robertson said.

Small-arms fire was so intense that it cut down a 22-inch oak tree (see Appendix B). Soldiers fired as many as 300 rounds—sometimes as many as 400. "Toward evening I had great difficulty in getting the balls down on account of the dirt and dust that had accumulated inside by my gun getting wet so often during the day," explained one Pennsylvanian. "The guns were so badly used up that they were condemned afterward, and we drew new ones."

When ammunition ran out or got wet, soldiers crushed each other's skulls with gun butts and used their bayonet freely. Others used spent rifles as spears. Observed one Federal: "The force with which [my comrade] threw it drove the bayonet entirely through [the Confederate's] chest, burying at least four inches of the muzzle of the gun in the breast of the Confederate, who uttered the most

unearthly yell I ever heard from human lips, as he fell over backward with the gun sticking in him."

The Battle of the Bloody Angle

They stabbed each other with swords. They hacked each other with hatchets. "The mud of the breastworks became a mass of torn bodies," said a Virginian.

"I was splashed over with brains and blood," a South Carolinian shuddered. "In stooping down or squatting to load, the mud, blood and brains mingled, would reach up to my waist, and my head and face were covered or spotted with the horrid paint."

"In that baleful glare men didn't look like men," said John Haley of Maine. Another soldier said men looked like fiends.

"[F]renzy seemed to possess the yelling demonic hordes on either side," Robertson added, "as soft-voiced tender hearted men in camp, sought like wild beasts, to destroy their fellow man."

*   *   *

"[W]ith every kind of shot and shell whistling over us, among us, in us and about us," said one Confederate, "it was as much as your life was worth to raise your head above the works."

The shells came courtesy of some 30 Union artillery pieces lined up along Landrum Lane and around the Landrum farm. At such close range—400 yards in some places—artillerists had a tough time firing over the heads of their own men without overshooting the Confederates. Mortars proved equally challenging because the mortar crews were inexperienced and ended up hitting Hancock's troops pinned outside the earthworks.

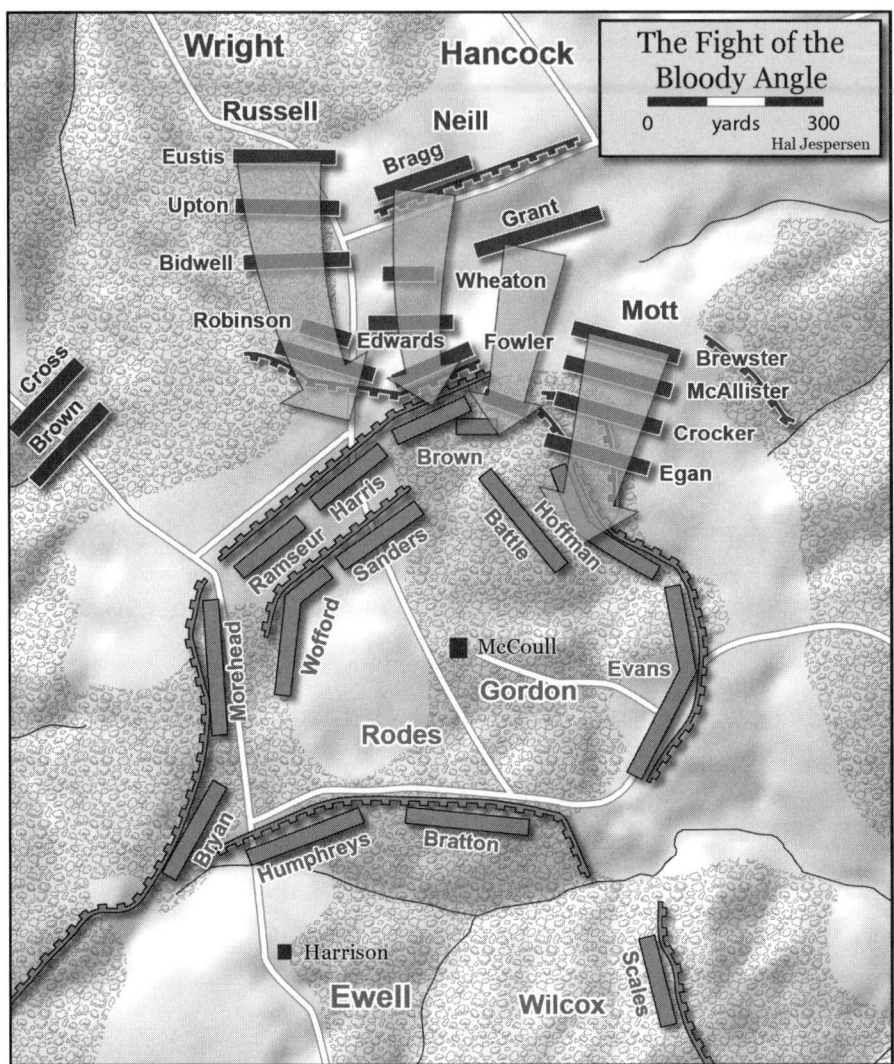

The Fight of the Bloody Angle

0 yards 300

Hal Jespersen

THE FIGHT OF THE BLOODY ANGLE

Lee traded lives for time, ordering his men to hold the salient while his engineers and survivors of his Second Corps constructed a new fallback position. Meanwhile, Federal troops from the II and VI Corps continued to pile into the fight. On the east face of the salient, Federals and Confederates settled into a grudging stalemate with parallel lines only feet apart. On the west face of the salient, however, the fight turned into a fierce hand-to-hand melee.

Finally, a young lieutenant, Richard Metcalf of the 5th U.S. Artillery, rolled a pair of cannons into the field directly in front of the Bloody Angle and began firing at nearly point-blank range. One cannon managed to get off nine rounds, the other 14, before Confederates gunned down the crews and horses.

Confusion reigned. Reports of white flags occasionally circulated but more often than not turned out to be false alarms or underhanded tricks. One Confederate and 12 of his blood-splattered men did jump the works and surrender to the 96th Pennsylvania. "The Devil couldn't stand it in there," the captain admitted.

Wounded soldiers could do little but ride out the storm—those who didn't literally got trampled into the mud. Edwin Moses of the 5th Maine was fortunate to have someone prop him, along with several other injured

Upton's brigade during the battle

soldiers, on a fence rail "to keep our shoulders above the mire into which the body had sunk by its own weight until, in some cases, the mud and water met over the hips."

Confederate Andrew Long, knocked unconscious early in Hancock's assault, thought he was going to die of thirst. "When I came to I crawled to a puddle of water through which men had been walking and fighting all day—and drank," he said. "All I wanted was water regardless of how dirty. There was mud, blood, and brains in this puddle."

Newly minted corps commander Horatio Wright, who'd been feeding troops into the melee all morning and afternoon, also sustained an injury. As the day wore on, Wright's initial optimism began to waiver, perhaps evaporating because he kept nipping at a bottle to dull the pain in his thigh. By the time Meade asked him to consolidate his position that evening, he snipped, "I have to say that I can't shorten my line a single foot."

The battlefield had become a hopeless tangle of soldiers, living and dead. Survivors were exhausted, hungry, and confused. Many were low on ammunition. Many were wounded. Stalemate persisted.

As night finally settled on the field, "the darkness was only broken by the flashing of the guns to light up the horrid scene . . . Every flash of the guns lights up the ghastly faces of the dead, with whom the ground is thickly strewn."

"It seemed to me," said Elisha Hunt Rhodes, "that the day would never pass away."

This sketch shows officers much closer to the front than they actually were. Hancock used the Landrum property for his headquarters for a time but eventually moved back to the Brown house when things got too hot.

*   *   *

By "the dark of the moon and a drizzling rain," Confederates finished work on the fallback line Lee had ordered across the base of the salient. At around 3:00 a.m., he sent word to the front for his men to begin their withdrawal. Singly and in pairs, the Confederates slipped away into the night. David Holt, a Mississippian, gazed behind him as he left: "It was still drizzling rain, and thin mist hung over everything.," he said. "There lay the tree cut down by bullets and the bloody ditch and the many dead and wounded. One wounded man was cursing, another praying to the Blessed Virgin. Many were crying for water, some begging to have the dead taken off them. I don't expect to go to hell, but if I do, I am sure that Hell can't beat that terrible scene."

As dawn broke on the morning of May 13, Federals discovered Lee's ruse and, in a rush, captured the last few hundred Confederates covering the withdrawal. At first, Federals felt exuberant that Lee had retreated—until a cautious pursuit revealed that Lee had not retreated at all, but rather now sat ensconced behind a set of works that looked even more formidable than those at the salient.

Feelings soured even further when soldiers really began to take in the carnage left behind. "[T]here has been no one spot like it in the whole war," one of them said.

The previous 24 hours had resulted in 17,000 casualties—some 8,000 Confederates and some 9,000 Federals—most of them strewn across the ground around the salient.

"The one exclamation of every man who looks on the spectacle," said one soldier, "is, 'God forbid that I should ever gaze on such a sight again.'"

At the Bloody Angle

The footpath that leads from the McCoull house comes out of the woods at about the same place that Brig. Gen. Nathaniel Harris' Mississippi brigade came charging as part of its counterattack on May 12. Once upon a time, the famed Stonewall Brigade had occupied this part of the Confederate line, but Hancock's overwhelming attack had literally wiped the brigade out of existence. By the time Harris arrived, Confederate counterattacks by Battle, Ramseur, and Perrin and driven the Federals back this far, and Harris pitched in to push them farther. To his right, McGowan's South Carolinians added their weight. A monument to McGowan's men, made of granite and dedicated in 2007, stands sentinel along the tree line to mark the highpoint of their advance.

A few yards down the path is a trail that leads into the woods to a set of reconstructed earthworks. Built by the C.C.C., they have since fallen into disrepair.

A coffin-like monument to McGowan's South Carolinians stands at the Bloody Angle.

On the outside of the angle stand monuments to the 49th New York and the 15th New Jersey. The New Jersey boys dedicated the monument here and one along the highway at Salem Church on May 12, 1909, inspired by a battlefield visit three years earlier. Then, they saw monuments to Stonewall Jackson and Uncle John Sedgwick and decided they should have monuments of their own. They even paid the state of New Jersey to pay for them. During the dedication ceremony at the Bloody Angle, they returned the battle flag of the 14th Georgia, which they had captured on that day 45 years earlier. Although the marker occupies a prominent place on the battlefield, the 15th New Jersey actually fought about 200 yards to the west, closer to Doles' Salient.

The 49th New York saw action at the Doles' Salient sector, but as part of Upton's attack force on May 10. On May 12, they came in as reinforcements funneled by the ravine into the maw of the Bloody Angle's worst fighting. They held their position, were eventually called away from the line, then went in again a little while later. Again on May 18, they attacked over the same ground as part of Grant's failed assault on Lee's last line. In October of 1902, they revisited the ground yet again—more than a thousand of them and their families—for the dedication of their monument.

The other marker at the angle is the concrete block that marks the site of 22-inch oak tree felled by small arms fire. (For more information, see sidebar.)

The reconstructed earthworks behind the Bloody Angle have fallen into disrepair.

A popular diorama of the Bloody Angle, installed in the Chancellorsville Visitor Center in the mid-1960s, depicted the carnage in clay. Note the oak tree in the scene.

Nature's Casualty at the Bloody Angle

BY KATHLEEN LOGOTHETIS

On May 12, 1864, when 17,000 men became casualties in and around the Bloody Angle, nature also suffered. Destruction of trees and foliage by small arms and artillery fire is often mentioned in soldiers' accounts of battle, particularly in the wooded areas of the Wilderness. Seeing trees fall during battle was not unusual, and several fell during the fighting at Spotsylvania, but one tree fall in particular received much attention.

Sometime between midnight and two o'clock in the morning, as the fighting raged on, a large oak fell inside the Confederate traverses about 50 yards east of the West Angle. B. F. Brown of the 1st South Carolina remembered the impact:

I was in the adjoining traverse and the top of the tree, when it fell, crashed into this traverse and I was literally covered with its limbs and leaves, but luckily sustained no further injury then the scraping of one of my ears by a small limb . . . One of the heavy limbs of the tree struck a comrade, who was near me, on the head with such force as to produce unconsciousness for several seconds.

What made this tree remarkable was its size and destruction: the 22-inch trunk had not been blasted by artillery fire, but was whittled away purely by Union musket and rifle fire.

Immediately after the battle, the tree was a curiosity. Members of the 1st South Carolina came back to view their position at the angle and examined the tree, as did General Lee and other officers.

A year later the war was over and as the Army of the Potomac marched north towards Washington, D.C., they stopped near the Spotsylvania battlefield. Nelson A. Miles, commander of the 1st Division, II Corps, which camped near the Landrum house, joined his men in sightseeing along the old battle lines. He and his staff discovered that the famous stump was gone, although the rest of the tree was still there and was quickly cut up by relic hunters. The whereabouts of the missing stump continued as a topic

Col. Nelson Miles refused to be stumped in his search.

of conversation as Miles and his staff went into town for dinner at the Spotswood Hotel. They asked the owner, a man by the name of Sanford, if he knew what had happened to the stump, but he expressed ignorance on its location.

Seems Sanford was not truthful, because as the group was leaving, an orderly reported to Miles that he had overheard a waiter tell a cook that he could tell the general about the stump's whereabouts. When the waiter was summoned, he revealed to the soldiers that the stump was locked in the hotel's smokehouse. Upon Sanford's refusal to unlock the door, the Union men broke it with an axe and "liberated" the stump.

Back in Washington, Miles presented the stump to Secretary of War Edwin Stanton, and it was kept in the Ordnance Museum under the War Department until 1888. Originally it was displayed at the entrance to the old War Department building near Pennsylvania Avenue. It was also displayed at the Centennial Celebration in Philadelphia in 1876 and made an appearance at the Chicago World's Fair in 1896.

On February 16, 1888, the "section of an oak cut down by musket balls near Spottsylvania Court House" was transferred, along with a "plaster model of equestrian statue of General McPherson" and "Mexican saddle and bridle, manufactured in Mexico for General Trevino," to the U.S. National Museum/Smithsonian. Today the stump is part of the Smithsonian Institution exhibit "The Price of Freedom: Americans at War," representing the horror of battle and the heroism of the men who fought.

On the battlefield, the site where the tree once stood is marked by a nondescript concrete block. "Site of 22-inche oak tree felled by small arms fire," an aluminum sign

The Bloody Angle stump now sits on display at the Smithsonian Institute in Washington, D.C.

The granite marker placed by Edward Stuart at the Bloody Angle sits next to the spot where the oak tree once stood. A different oak tree grows near the block now.

The granite block, now bare, was once adorned by a plaque that identified the stump's location.

next to it reads. According to park historian Don Pfanz, the block is all that remains of three markers installed by one-time landowner Edward Stuart. "Stuart had a great interest in the battle, and on his own initiative he erected three simple stones marking the sites of the East Angle, the West Angle, and Bloody Angle Oak," Pfanz writes. "In a small, informal gathering held on July 7, 1931, Stuart and a few friends set the markers in place. Today just the base of the Bloody Angle Oak marker remains. The East and West Angle markers vanished sometime after 1955. It is not clear who removed them or for what reason."

⟶ TO STOP 7

At this point, whether you've been walking or driving, you should return to your vehicle to continue the driving tour. Because of the configuration of park roads, the tour will go out of sequence compared to the chronological narrative of events. This will give you an opportunity to explore the ground associated with the Federal assaults on May 18. That action is covered in chapter 13.

Visitors who explored via the walking tour may wish to skip driving tour stop 6 (since they've seen it by foot) and go directly to stop 7. For those visitors, follow Grant Drive to the Y-intersection of bear right onto Anderson Drive.

For visitors parked at the McCoull house, return down McCoull Lane to Gordon Drive. Turn right, and drive for 400 feet. At the "Y," bear left onto Anderson Drive.

Once on Anderson Drive, follow it for 0.3 miles. Park in one of the spaces in front of the reconstructed earthworks.

GPS: N 38° .21436 W 77° .60772

The Spotswood Hotel (top), also known as the Sanford Hotel, sits at the center of Spotsylvania Court House. It is now a private office building (below).

⟶ TO STOP 8

For battlefield visitors at stop 6 who would like to stick with the chronological narrative, turn left onto Gordon Drive and follow it (which will eventually turn into Burnside Drive) 1.3 miles to the parking area for Heth's Salient.

For battlefield visitors who have followed the driving tour to stop 7, retrace your route along Anderson Drive for 0.3 miles, and take a right at the "Y." The view of the open fields on the right offers a good perspective of the terrain Federal troops tried to cross during their attacks on May 18. Continue along Gordon Drive 1.4 miles. On the right, you will see parking spaces along the right side of the road in front of a small black monument.

GPS: N 38° .21407 W 77° .58780

Heth's Salient

CHAPTER ELEVEN

MAY 12, 1864

Major General Ambrose Everett Burnside had been the shortest-tenured commander of the Army of the Potomac. His 77 days were marked with failure and political infighting, infamously crowned by the debacle at Fredericksburg in December, 1862. In disgrace, he was shipped west to command the Department of the Ohio, but there, in the winter of 1863-64, a remarkable thing happened: he redeemed his reputation during the Confederate siege of Knoxville, Tennessee.

In fact, Burnside's success impressed Grant enough that, when Grant ascended to the position of general-in-chief, he recalled Burnside and his old IX Corps back to the Eastern Theater of the war. They arrived just in time to participate in the second day's action in the Wilderness—where Burnside performed poorly. He had exhibited "a case of the slows," a fellow officer remarked.

The 39-year-old native of Indiana, known for his stylish cheek whiskers, was a good-natured man, personally well-liked by almost everyone who knew him. An 1847 graduate of West Point, he'd fought in the Civil War since First Bull Run, where he showed flashes of brilliance. Later, he scored successes along the North Carolina coast.

Things began to change following the battle of Antietam. Burnside's close friend, army commander Maj. Gen. George McClellan, blamed the bewhiskered Indianian for the Federal army's failure to destroy the Army of Northern Virginia. Ironically, Burnside took over as army commander shortly thereafter, inheriting McClellan's inept supply and logistics system, which then left the Army

Maj. Gen. Ambrose E. Burnside (inset)

The course of their attack took Burnside's men through a pair of low, swampy areas.

101

Maj. Gen. Harry Heth

Burnside was to attack in concert with Hancock to relieve pressure on the II Corps.

of the Potomac on the wrong side of the Rappahannock River outside Fredericksburg.

The battle there in mid-December represented the most lopsided loss the army faced in the entire war. And then there was the politicking within the army: behind Burnside's back, several officers went up to Washington to tell tales of woe about Burnside's reign as commander. By the time Lincoln cut through all the infighting and allowed Burnside's army to move against the enemy, Mother Nature stepped in and crushed Burnside's winter campaign, an ill-fated expedition that became known as the Mud March.

Despite the many downs and ups, Burnside remained one of the highest-ranking generals in the Union army. Because of that high rank, Burnside and his corps were not part of the Army of the Potomac when they returned to the east because Burnside would have outranked army commander George Meade. Instead, the IX Corps acted as an independent command that reported directly to Grant.

The command structure proved unwieldy, though, because it made it difficult to coordinate attacks between three commanders: Grant, Meade, and Burnside.

On the afternoon of May 12, for instance, Grant ordered Burnside to help Meade break the Confederate line back open. Lee's morning counterattacks had all but sealed off the Mule Shoe's tip, so Grant wanted Burnside to crack open its base. Burnside targeted a second small salient, known as Heth's Salient, which got its name from the Confederate division commander, Maj. Gen. Harry Heth, who defended that stretch of the line. Heth's Salient jutted from the Confederate line approximately one mile south east of the tip of the Mule Shoe.

May 12 had already been busy for the IX Corps. That morning, one of its divisions had hit the Mule Shoe in coordination with Hancock's assault. Although the attack held Confederates in place, preventing Lee from using them as reinforcements, Burnside's men couldn't crack the line. Otherwise, Burnside seemed content to pound the Southern trenches with his artillery.

As Burnside's men approached Heth's Salient, Confederates swung around to the Federal flank and caught them by surprise in this open ground.

Grant wanted more. Along the Federal right, V Corps commander Gouverneur Warren remained immobile, convinced his men faced further doom. Only when Grant threatened to replace him did he move, and then only sluggishly.

Near 2:00 p.m., Grant turned to his left to prod the sluggish Burnside into action, too. "Push the enemy with all your might," he ordered. "We must not fail."

Burnside organized men from two divisions into an attack column and launched them forward toward the ridge where the Confederates awaited. Two streams also cut through Burnside's path, creating a low marshy area his men had to cut through. Southern artillery battered them as they approached.

Suddenly a sledgehammer blow hit the left of Burnside's assault column.

Robert E. Lee, not one to sit behind earthworks and passively allow the enemy to attack time and again, had already looked toward Heth's Salient as the next front to open an offensive of his own. Earlier in the afternoon, Lee had ridden into the salient and spied Burnside's line sitting idly atop a bald hill near the Beverley house. Lee ordered his men to launch an attack against Burnside's left flank in the hope that it would relieve the pressure then being applied on Ewell's men in the Mule Shoe. Dislodging the Federal army from its current position might then allow Lee to go on the offensive.

That Burnside launched an attack almost simultaneously proved providential for Lee. He just happened to have an attack force already prepared to meet the threat.

As Burnside's men strode up and out of the marsh, 10 Confederate regiments slammed into their left. "It was terrible, terrible, yet exciting," a Confederate enthused.

The battle was brief but vicious, even deteriorating into a hand-to-hand melee for a few moments. "It literally rained shot and shell all around us and our comrades were falling on every side by scores," a Michigander wrote.

The Federals finally fell back to the hill from whence they came. Three full Federal batteries poured canister fire into the Confederate lines to hold back the pursuit. Artillery from both sides resumed pounding each other's positions.

As at the Mule Shoe and at Laurel Hill, stalemate gripped the field.

At Heth's Salient

Monument to the 17th Michigan

Opposite: The tip of Heth's Salient

It might seem, at first, odd to raise a monument to a unit that had 150 of its men taken prisoner and its flag captured here. That's what happened to the 17th Michigan on May 12, sent against Heth's Salient in an attempt to alleviate pressure on Federal troops hanging on for dear life in the Mule Shoe. In all, the unit lost 189 of the 225 men it carried into battle. Three of the unit's survivors were awarded the Medal of Honor for their attempts, unsuccessful as they were, at recapturing their lost flag. To commemorate that bravery, the 17th Michigan re-enactors dedicated the monument in 1997.

Some of the best-preserved earthworks in the park are at Heth's Salient. A hiking trail used to stretch into the woods from behind the Michigan monument all the way up to the salient's tip, but the path has since fallen into disuse. Visitors who brave the hillside in the summer should be aware of the presence of snakes and ticks.

→ **TO STOP 9**

Follow Burnside Drive 0.7 miles to the parking area for the Fredericksburg Road and park your vehicle there.

GPS: N 38.21124 W 77.57741

Myer's Hill

CHAPTER TWELVE

MAY 13, 1864

Grant didn't believe the first reports that reached him on the morning of May 13. "I do not infer the enemy are making a stand but simply covering a retreat," he believed, "which must necessarily have been slow with such roads and so dark a night as they had last night." But further reconnaissance left no doubt about the Confederate position. "[T]hey are still before us in force," Grant conceded.

The new center looked strong. The Confederate left along Laurel Hill had proven nearly impregnable, too. Aside from lackluster attacks by Burnside against Heth's Salient, Grant had not made any moves against the Confederate right. Action had all focused to the north and west of the Court House. Shifting to the north and east, instead, might offer a way to get at Lee.

At the very least, the new position would allow Grant to consolidate his supply line from Fredericksburg, which alone would make the effort worthwhile. It would also put him a few steps closer to the Telegraph Road, the main north-south artery that led to Richmond.

Grant cut orders to move the V and VI corps away from Laurel Hill past the backside of the Federal army, similar to Hancock's maneuver on the night of May 11. The two corps would then leapfrog past Burnside's IX Corps and extend the Federal left past the Fredericksburg Road. Hancock's men at the old Mule Shoe would then be the new right flank of the army, Wright's men the new left.

Grant hoped to have the two corps in their new places by dawn, at which time he wanted to launch an attack against the unsuspecting Lee and his presumably weak right flank.

More rain fell. Already saturated roads became quagmires. The march, set to begin in the evening, bogged down. "[I]t was the hardest nights march we ever endured as it was hot-muggy, rained, dark," one of Warren's men said. "The pioneers had cut a road through the brushy woods and the stubs would trip, as the mud was deep and

Only a few trenchlines remain atop Myer's Hill.

107

we found 2 streams." (It's curious to wonder what Burnside, the victim of a catastrophic mud march in January of 1863, must have thought as he watched the V and VI corps slog past his men.)

By dawn, Warren reported 2,500 men on line and ready. The rest remained mired on the road. Meade and Grant were frustrated and furious.

Warren surprised them with a small flare for the offensive.

Three-quarters of a mile from Spotsylvania Court House rose Myers Hill, "a bold, round hill on the south bank of the [Ni], upon which was a well-appointed farmer's dwelling." The hill, Warren reasoned, could serve as the perfect point to mass artillery for a bombardment on Lee's headquarters in town and the Confederate line around it. A token force of Confederate horsemen held the hill—the 9th Virginia Cavalry, a unit comprised of men from in and around Spotsylvania County.

Two veteran regiments, the 91st Pennsylvania and 14th New York, moved toward the hill. Both units had opened the battles in both the Wilderness and outside Spotsylvania. After a quick fight, the Federals captured the hill.

The Ni River had steep banks that made it difficult to cross. Two days of rain made the crossing even harder.

Reinforcements, including newly minted Brig. Gen. Emory Upton, rushed in to consolidate the Federal position. All felt fatigued from the long night march and the muddy, difficult struggle across the Ni River, not far from the hill's base.

Atop the hill, Upton oversaw construction of a defensive line. On the south slope, he deployed the four regiments of his brigade, with two New Jersey regiments near the Myer's house as a reserve. Scouts climbed into the attic of the home and cut holes in the roof so spotters could use it as a lookout. Troops set up makeshift earthworks and barricades, using much of the wood from other parts of the house in their constructions.

*   *   *

From his position south of Myer's Hill, Third Corps commander Jubal Early had watched all this, and his blood was up. Yankee artillery atop the hill would make his position untenable, and that would not do. Early put together a mixed force of artillery, infantry, and cavalry and set out from his trenches to do battle.

In effect, this is exactly what Grant wanted, albeit on a smaller scale. He wanted at least a portion of Lee's army in the open where he could get at it. Unfortunately, Grant didn't yet have enough Federals in the area to take advantage of the opportunity.

Lee's "Bad Old Man," Maj. Gen. Jubal Early

Upton, tucked upon the hill, received word from his spotters that Early was coming. With two brigades of infantry, a brigade of mostly dismounted cavalry, and four pieces of artillery, the weight of the makeshift Confederate line was too much for Upton's men, who had seen heavy action over the last five days and whose ranks were badly depleted. The Federal line crumbled. "We gave the yell and they commenced skedaddling," one Southerner said.

Meanwhile, near the bottom of the hill's north face, Meade was riding up to see his new prize. Suddenly Upton's men came "skedaddling" past, with Confederates hot on their heels. "Gen. Meade had to gallop for it," said his aide, Theodore Lyman, "and not being familiar with the paths came quite near enough being cut off!"

Infuriated by the episode—and likely embarrassed by it, too—Meade ordered Wright to retake the hill, authorizing him to use his entire corps and the entire V Corps, too.

"[W]hen all was ready the bugle sounded the charge and we broke from cover like quarter horses and with a volley of cheers mounted the hill," a member of the 12th U.S. infantry said. "The rebs were lying on the other side to avoid our shells which were hissing and exploding around the crest and when they heard our cheers supposed a mighty force was coming and so they ran like the devil."

Dusk soon settled in. The hill belonged, in the end, to the Army of the Potomac, and Meade began using it at once as a base of operations against Lee's right flank. Of more consequence, though, was the Fredericksburg Road. Supplies could flow more freely and, should he chose to do so, Grant now had an open route that could take him to Richmond.

A radio tower marks the location of Myer's Hill for modern travelers. The hill itself lies outside the NPS boundary and so, as privately owned land, is not accessible to the public. Ironically, the Park Service once had the opportunity to buy portions of the property but turned it down. For a time, land acquisition policy steered away from properties that weren't contiguous with property already owned by the park. Myer's Hill, isolated as it is, presented management challenges. Since then, preservation groups have eyed the property on several occasions but have been unable to come to any deals. A single road runs along part of Myer's Hill: Gunnery Road, which branches off Massaponax Church Road. From the road, just before it passes under the towering power lines, visitors can see the remains of the trenches Upton's men constructed. The earthworks can be seen on both sides of the road, which cuts diagonally across them.

→ TO STOP 10

Follow Burnside Drive to its intersection with Route 208 (Court House Road). Turn right onto Route 208 and follow it 0.3 miles to the traffic light. Turn left onto Old Court House Road and follow it for 0.6 miles into Spotsylvania Court House. Park in the courthouse complex on the right.

GPS: N 38° .20139 W 77° .58875

Mud and Maneuver

CHAPTER THIRTEEN

MAY 14-17, 1864

Rain. Rain. Rain.

And mud.

"The whole country is a sea of mud," a Federal artillerist wrote.

"An ordinary rain, lasting for a day or two, does not embarrass troops," said Grant's aide Horace Porter.

> *But when the storm continues for a week it becomes one of the most serious obstacles in a campaign. The men can secure no proper shelter and no comfortable rest; their clothing has no chance to dry; and a tramp of a few miles through tenacious mud requires as much exertion as an ordinary day's march. Tents become saturated and weighted with water, and draft animals have increased loads and heavier roads over which to haul them. Dry wood cannot be found; cooking becomes difficult; the men's spirits are affected by the gloom, and even the most buoyant natures become disheartened.*

Grant certainly felt so—and it made him antsy. "The heavy rains for the past three days have rendered the roads so impassable that but little will be done until there is a change of weather, unless the enemy should attack, which they have exhibited little inclination to do for the last week," he wrote to Washington.

He put the time to such use as he could, handling administrative matters. On the 13th, for instance, he put forth Meade's name for promotion along with William Tecumseh Sherman's—Grants trusted successor in the Western Theater. "General Meade has more than met my most sanguine expectations," Grant wrote. "He and Sherman are the fittest officers for large commands I have come in contact with. If their services can be rewarded by promotion to the ranks of major-generals in the regular army the honor would be worthily bestowed, and I would feel personally gratified. I would not like to see one of these promotions at this time without seeing both."

May 11 marked the first day of rain that would continue on and off for the rest of the month. Grant, on the offense, was hampered by the mud far more than Lee, hunkered in a defensive position.

He might also have given consideration to the problems of communication that continued to crop up between Meade's army and Burnside's independent command of IX Corps, a situation he would finally remedy on May 24—the day after Burnside's 40th birthday, as it would happen—by officially folding Burnside's corps into Meade's command structure.

Although much speculation has occurred in postwar writings about the relationship between Meade and Grant, such actions demonstrate Grant's faith in the "goddamned google-eyed snapping turtle" who commanded the Union's premier army. Grant would hardly have recommended Meade for promotion or given him more men to command had he been unhappy with the Pennsylvanian.

Grant also used the lull to order up more reinforcements. The continual grind of the campaign had thus far depleted his ranks by some 31,000 men. A dispatch to Washington soon mobilized 30,000 replacements who began making their way toward Spostylvania Country immediately.

But mostly, Grant kept studying his maps and studying Lee's fortifications. There had to be some way to get at the old Gray Fox—but how?

* * *

Lee didn't have the same luxury of reinforcements that Grant did. "We are outnumbered and constant labor is impairing the efficiency of the men," Lee wrote to President Jefferson Davis.

Major General John C. Breckenridge's victory at New Market in the Shenandoah Valley that very day, May 15, would soon make reinforcements available. Major General George Pickett, who now had Benjamin Butler's army bottled up south of the James River, would also be able to send some. It would be days, though, before any of those troops would reach Lee.

Just as immediately, what Lee needed was information. With most of his cavalry gone—and with his brilliant cavalry chief, Jeb Stuart, now dead following an engagement at Yellow Tavern (see Appendix A)—he had to depend on his infantry to get it.

First, he sent the First Corps division of Brig. Gen. Joseph Kershaw forward on a reconnaissance in force. Moving carefully, they eventually stumbled into the tail end of Hancock's corps, which now made up the extreme right of the Army of the Potomac. Kershaw launched into them, battering the already-battered division of David Birney, which had suffered terribly at the Mule Shoe. Grant had ordered the II Corps to move eastward toward the Fredericksburg Road, and Birney had been left in place to guard the movement. Birney held on long enough to let the rest of the corps slip away, but Kershaw learned what he needed to. Satisfied, the South Carolinian withdrew.

Brig. Gen. Joseph Kershaw

The area where Rosser's Confederate cavalry tangled with Ferraro's U.S.C.T. regiments is all in private hands and remains uninterpreted. Coming from the direction of Todd's Tavern, a motorist will pass the Wilderness Elementary School on the left and then will round a couple gentle curves in the road before coming to the ground. A housing development on the left clogs the view, but the open fields on the right offer a bit of a glimpse of the ground the U.S.C.T. crossed. An account of that engagement, which we draw from here, can be read in F. S. Bowley's *A Boy Lieutenant*. The intersection itself, well protected during the battle, has a tricky configuration today. A left-hand turn will lead to the Lee-Jackson Bivouac site on the Chancellorsville Battlefield and, a mile beyond, to the Chancellorsville intersection itself. A right-hand turn will eventually lead toward modern Route 3 and a T-intersection with Gordon Road. A right on Gordon will lead back to the Brock Road and the Spotsylvania Battlefield.

Little did Lee realize the lost opportunity. With a little more muscle, he might have finished off one of the Army of the Potomac's finest divisions.

* * *

Aside from Kershaw's foray, Lee had a cavalry detachment at his disposal commanded by Brig. Gen. Thomas Rosser, which he sent on a sweeping arc north up the Brock Road. At Todd's Tavern, he turned east on Catharpin Road with an eye on the Orange Plank Road. The muddy roads made for slow progress.

En route, Rosser's men stumbled upon the 2nd Ohio Cavalry. "If the fool Johnnies had only kept their throats closed, they would have bagged the regiment almost entire," one Ohioan later said. Instead, with a hoot and a holler, the Confederate cavalry charged in. The Ohioans scattered.

Most of the Buckeyes fled north toward the Alrich farm, located at the intersection of Catharpin Road and the Orange Plank Road. There, a division of United States Colored Troops (U.S.C.T.) attached to the IX Corps guarded supply trains and a field hospital. Relegated to the rear of the army, the U.S.C.T. regiments had never before seen combat. "I think Gen Grant don't intend to put us in the fight unless he is short of men," one of them lamented.

The fact was, no one quite knew what to do with the U.S.C.T. Grant worried about their safety, fearing that Southerners would massacre any black troops they found. Conventional "wisdom" held that black troops would cave under the pressure of combat and run away. Others believed blacks would fight like demons because they had the most on the line and something to prove. Others worried that, regardless of the U.S.C.T.'s performance, any actual or perceived misuse of black troops could have unpredictable political ramifications in what was certain to be a close election year.

Suddenly, with a few hundred Confederate cavalry bearing

Brig. Gen. Thomas Rosser

113

Brig. Gen. Edward Ferrero

Sgt. Nimrod Burke of the 23rd U.S.C.T., one of the units that confronted Rosser's cavalry

down on them hell bent for leather, none of that mattered.

Brigadier General Edward Ferrero, a former New York City dance instructor who'd proven himself an effective combat leader, mobilized his men. As they fell into line and began forward, one of their officers said, "Now just imagine you are hunting for coons, and keep your eyes open." One of the soldiers laughed. "'Pears like 'twas de coons doin' de huntin' dis time," he said.

The harried Ohioans, seeing salvation at hand, greeted them enthusiastically. "It did us good to see the long line of glittering bayonets approach, although those who bore them were Blacks," one Buckeye wrote, "and as they came nearer they were greeted by loud cheers."

The green troops almost made a disastrous blunder as they deployed: the 30th U.S.C.T. threw out a line of skirmishers that included their color company. That would have put their flags too close to the enemy. The capture of the colors would have been a powerful embarrassment to not only the regiment but to the reputation of the fledgling U.S.C.T. as a whole. The men quickly rectified their mistake, though, and went into battle in fine formation.

Rosser's men, seeing they suddenly had a fight on their hands, dismounted in the forest on the edge of the field. They were among the best cavalrymen in the Confederacy, but against a division of infantry, even green infantry, they stood little chance. One volley from the Federals convinced the horsemen to mount back up and pull out—a prudent choice on Rosser's part considering the circumstances. He faced an unknown force behind enemy lines, with muddy roads as their only escape route and thunderstorms darkening the sky.

Rosser didn't just retreat back to Spotsylvania, though. His men continued to gather intelligence, and at one point, they brushed against Birney's pickets, who'd already had a very, very long day. Rosser never mentioned the U.S.C.T. in his final report, referring only to a "small force of infantry."

But Ferrero's real victory came not just because his men had turned back Rosser's raid. For the first time in the war, black troops had seen combat against Lee's Army of Northern Virginia. And they had won.

It had been, Ferrero later crowed, "a perfect rout."

At Spotsylvania Court House

Lee moved his headquarters into the crossroads village of Spotsylvania Court House, a location later marked in 1903 by James Power Smith. A Presbyterian minister in Fredericksburg, Smith had served on the staff of Stonewall Jackson during the war. He assisted with the placement of the Jackson monument along the Orange Turnpike at Chancellorsville, and later he erected 10 granite blocks at other key spots on the area's battlefields. One of those spots marked Lee's headquarters during the army commander's time in the village. The monument sits at the heart of the village on the front lawn of the courthouse, close to the intersection of the Brock Road and the old Fredericksburg Road.

As Grant continued to try and outmaneuver Lee, Lee spent much of his time here figuring out how to counter those movements. He inspected his maps, inspected his troops, inspected his fortifications. But always he looked for ways, too, to strike a blow, although the occasion never presented itself. It was to near this area where the Confederate artillery from the Mule Shoe was ordered to on the evening of May 11. From here, the gunners would make their way back in the mud and rain to the chaos that was the fight for the Bloody Angle.

Third Corps commander Jubal Early also had his headquarters in the village, at the old Spotswood Hotel, which now serves as an office building. Visitors downtown can also see the new courthouse, which sits on the site of the old courthouse and is adorned with Doric columns from the original structure. The old jail, whose exterior walls are two feet thick, is also downtown.

To the northeast of town, visitors can find the Spotsylvania Confederate Cemetery. Because many of the Confederates had "home field advantage," many of them had families who came to retrieve their bodies. Others could be more easily shipped home because the Confederacy's infrastructure still remained relatively stable in the east. Still, more than 600 Confederates killed in the battles in Spotsylvania County found their final resting place in here. More were buried in the Fredericksburg City Cemetery. Union soldiers who'd been buried in field graves, meanwhile, were later reinterred in Fredericksburg National Cemetery, beside the Fredericksburg Battlefield Visitor Center.

A marker denotes the area of Lee's HQ, with the former Spotswood Hotel in the background.

The original jailhouse

⟶ TO STOP 11

Turn left onto Old Court House Road. After 0.3 miles, you will pass the Confederate cemetery on the right, where you may choose to stop (GPS: N 38° .20286 W 77° .58342).

After another 0.3 miles, you will reach the intersection with Route 208. Turn right and go 1.7 miles, then turn left onto Bloomsbury Lane (use caution crossing traffic). Follow Bloomsbury Lane 0.3 miles and turn right onto Agnes Lane; follow Agnes Lane 0.2 miles and turn left onto Pond View Lane; follow Pond View Lane 0.2 miles to its intersection with South Harris Farm Road. Park in the pull off directly in front of the intersection

More than 600 soldiers lay interred in the Spotsylvania Confederate Cemetery.

GPS: N 38° .23379 W 77° .56844

115

CONFEDERATE
TRENCHES
Lees Final Line

Engineering Over Infantry

CHAPTER FOURTEEN

MAY 18, 1864

For five and a half days, rain drenched the armies and muddied the landscape, but on May 17, the sun once more appeared. It almost tantalized Grant, eager as he was for action but hampered by the mire. "The conditions of the roads was such that nothing was done on the 17th," he wrote.

But battle was coming—and soon. Meade knew it, too.  "To-morrow we shall begin fighting again, with, I trust, some decided result," Meade wrote to his wife, "for it is hardly natural to expect men to maintain without limit the exhaustion of such a protracted struggle as we have been carrying on."

Grant had decided on a massive assault down the Fredericksburg Road, which is why he ordered Hancock's corps to move east—the movement Kershaw had stumbled into on May 17. On further consideration, though, Grant decided on an assault down the Massaponax Road, instead, a little farther to the south. Either route would have taken him into Lee's right flank.

However, with the information Kershaw and Rosser had gathered, Lee knew the Federal army had concentrated along the Fredericksburg Road. Armed with his new knowledge, Lee gleaned Grant's motives and countered by strengthening that sector of his line. When Horatio Wright sent a pair of regiments on a reconnaissance mission there on May 17, Wright found out just how tight Lee's grip in that area was.

So Grant began to plan anew.

Had he cavalry available to gather information, Grant's

Confederates used the rainy days to fortify. (inset)

Heaps of stones mark the four corners of the former Harrison House.

117

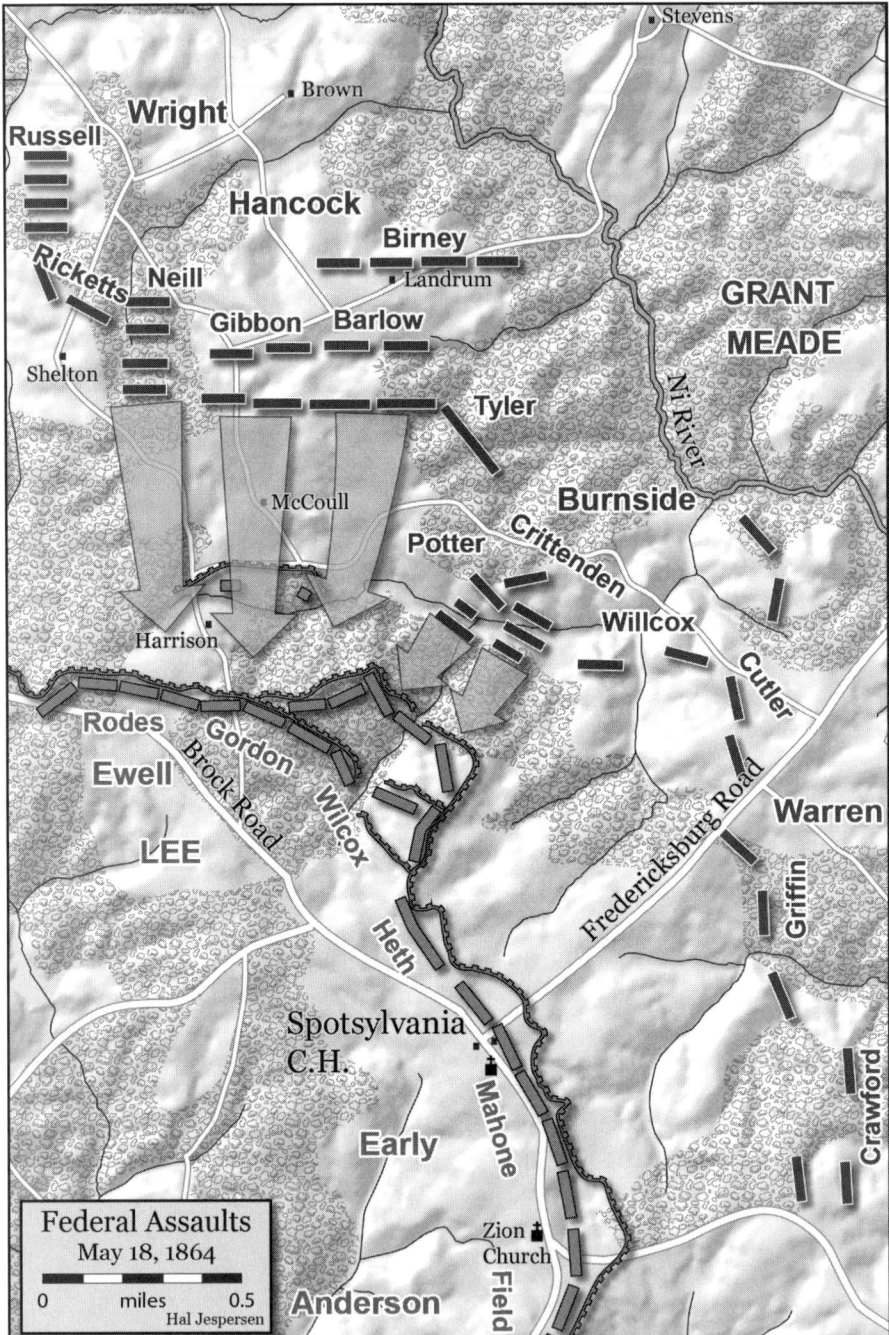

FEDERAL ASSAULTS—On May 18, Grant launched an attack against Lee's left—which, by then, was the area near the former Mule Shoe—assuming that Confederates had weakened their line there in order to strengthen their right. However, the men of the Second Corps occupied that stretch of the line. They'd spent the days since their drubbing on May 12 strengthening their line, creating the most extensive works yet seen in the Eastern Theater. For all its power, Grant's assault force could barely get within rifle range because Confederate artillery had such an advantage.

118

planning would have gone smoother, but Sheridan was still gallivanting around Richmond. Instead, Grant had to rely on his gut: the Army of the Potomac had shifted its center of gravity to the Fredericksburg Road, and the Army of Northern Virginia seemed to have done the same . . .

Grant turned his eyes back to the old battlefield of the 10th and 12th.

"The Second and Sixth Corps are to return to the old ground on the right and pitch in there," his men learned. They would march overnight—the II and VI corps— and launch the attack at 4:30 a.m. over the very ground Hancock had assaulted on May 12.

"[G]reat things are hoped from it by Grant," a Federal diarist wrote. "I fear he will not find Lee asleep."

* * *

Asleep or not, Confederates in that sector of the line were plenty well rested. Since turning his attention eastward on the morning of May 13, Grant had not exerted any pressure on Richard Ewell's Second Corps. The corps, now occupying its new line along Harrison Hill on the Confederate left, had essentially done nothing for five days other than rest, refit, and strengthen their works. "[F]earful of a repetition of the terrible assault, the garrison worked with the energy of perseverance, almost of despair," a Union observer later learned—the hard way.

The front of Ewell's line bristled with "acres of

Confederate fortifications became fortress-like. They are clearly the precursor to the trench warfare of WWI.

Federals try to sweep across the open field.

impenetrable abatis," and in the open fields and ravines in front, slashings of all sorts blocked the approach. Inside the line, heavy log reinforcements held up earthen walls, and traverses offered protection from enfilading fire and rallying points for any possible breakthroughs. Artillerists manned pieces placed at strategic points along the line.

Grant had no way to know he was about to assault the strongest field fortifications constructed in the east to date.

The battlefield featured one other morbid addition: the black, bloated bodies of soldiers slain in battle on the 12th, washed out of their shallow graves by days of rain. "The stench which arose from them was so sickening and terrible that many of the men and officers became deathly sick from it," one Federal soldier wrote.

Hancock had attacked over this same ground days earlier, to sweeping success. This time, he aligned only two of his four divisions into formation, then added a third from the VI Corps—the only VI Corps division that could make it onto the field in a timely fashion. The rest of Wright's corps remained on the road.

When Hancock attacked, Burnside, too, was to attack the area north of Heth's Salient to tie down any possible reinforcements from that area. At the same time, artillery from all three corps would hammer away at the butternut trenches.

"Early on the morning of Wednesday, May 18, the whizzing of shells announced that the second great battle of Spottsylvania Court House had been commenced," wrote a VI Corps officer.

"We started in line of battle before daylight and marched through the woods and brush towards the enemy," wrote Rhode Islander Elisha Hunt Rhodes. Mud hampered the advance, which took troops through the ravaged trenches that outlined the old Mule Shoe then up past the McCoull property. There, two companies of Confederate skirmishers surprised them.

After recovering from that nasty trap, Rhodes said, "we came in sight of their line of forts and made a charge, but it was of no use, for their Artillery cut our men down in heaps." Confederate Brig. Gen. Armistead Long brought 29

Ruins of the Harrison house

Federal division commander John Gibbon and his staff watch the assault.

cannon to bear on the advancing Federals, firing both case and canister shot at them. Federal artillery countered—and the largest artillery bombardment in the Eastern Theater since Gettysburg commenced.

"Who does not believe it seemed a lifetime to many of those men, who, with bent body an erect bayonet, won their perilous way, foot by foot, through whistling balls, bursting shells gnawing grape," wondered W. T. G. Morton, a Union surgeon.

At the center of the Federal formation was the brigade of Col. Matthew Murphy, which had joined the Army of the Potomac just the day before. Murphy's men struggled valiantly to push ahead of Hancock's other brigades, but to no avail. Murphy fell wounded, and his brigade, unsupported, was shot to pieces.

Another brigade refused to enter the fray at all—the veteran Philadelphia brigade of John Gibbon's division. Gibbon hadn't even missed them at first. When he did, he ordered them in, but his brigadier refused to go. Their act of defiance would contribute to his dismissal, and the disbandment of the brigade, in the months ahead.

The entire Union attack floundered. "Smoke and mist hung pale, heavy, and motionless over the troops," Morton said.

"For a few minutes all was observed in mystery," wrote a Federal artillerist:

Moments seemed like hours. Then the cheering ceased and dark masses of our men were seen through the openings in the uprising smoke returning as they went but with awfully suggestive gaps in their ranks. The assault had failed. Soon the smoke cleared away and disclosed the ground for long distances thickly strewn with our dead and dying men.

"It was an awfully grand spectacle," he concluded, "one often repeated around that ground which has been justly styled 'Bloody Spotsylvania.'"

*   *   *

From Anderson Drive, looking across the open attack field Federals had to cross on May 18, moving from left to right. They barely made it within rifle range.

In front of Heth's Salient, Burnside fared no better.

The ham-fisted Maj. Gen. Thomas Crittenden, a politician turned general, and Maj. Gen. Robert Potter, one of the heroes of Antietam, led Burnside's divisions into battle. Their assault came to an abrupt end when they ran into two sturdy brigades of North Carolinas and Georgians. "[T]he limbs, and even the trees, were cut down like grass, and the place was most decidedly uncomfortable," a Massachusetts lieutenant wrote. Although the IX Corps men made it closer to the Confederate lines than their counterparts in the II and VI corps, they still did not break through.

By 10 a.m. Grant had seen enough. The Confederate line at Spotsylvania Court House was far too strong to breach.

"No attempt ever more completely failed," lamented one Bay Stater. "We went in, lost some men and came out again—that is all there was to it!"

A New Jersey soldier disagreed, but only in the outcome. "[W]e advanced," he said, "over essentially the same ground we did on the 12th without accomplishing anything except to meet with a very considerable loss." Indeed, the Northern losses exceeded 1,500, compared to some 250 casualties.

"After the fight," cringed one Southern cannoneer, "the battle field presented a horrible spectacle, some having their heads and limbs torn away from their bodies."

That night, the sun went down red, said Morton:

The smoke of the battle of more than two hundred thousand men destroying each other with villainous saltpeter through all the long hours of a long day, filled the valleys, and rested on the hills of all this wilderness, hung in lurid haze all around the horizon, and built a dense canopy overhead, beneath which this grand army of freedom was preparing to rest against the morrow.

Along Lee's last line

Chronologically, this portion of the narrative falls on May 18, but because of the considerable amount of maneuvering the armies did beginning on May 13, coupled with the one-way roads of the Park, the easiest way to see this ground follows a stop at the Bloody Angle.

By the parking area, a set of reconstructed earthworks serves as the road's dead end. Soldiers stacked logs atop one another and then piled dirt on the outside from the trenches they dug on the inside. Typically, an additional log called a "head log" was placed a few inches above the top of the wall; this protected infantrymen from headshots as they stood in the trench and shot through the gap.

Standing in the trench and facing the logs, one can see the Confederate earthworks stretch through the open glen to the left. A second set branches away to run parallel to the road. This "Y" in the line is the spot where the Mule Shoe began its long bend away from the otherwise straight line. Lee ordered this new line to stretch across the base of the salient. It became known as "Lee's last line."

A footpath runs from the parking area along Lee's last line all the way out to the former site of the Harrison house. In places, a second line of earthworks splits away from the first. Engineers tried to take advantage of the topography, which offered enough elevation for two lines, which allowed Second Corps commander Richard Ewell to stack more men in those particular areas.

The path leaves the woods and runs down into a dip before cresting at the ruins of Edgar Harrison's house. Rock piles mark the corners of the foundation. Lee had his headquarters here prior to the collapse of the Mule Shoe.

At the end of Anderson Drive, near the trailhead that runs along Lee's last line, reconstructed earthworks give visitors a sense of the fortifications that have since given way to time. The juncture of the original line that formed the salient and the final line can be clearly seen in the lightly forested glen near the parking area.

→ TO STOP 8

From here, the driving tour goes to Heth's Salient, covered in chapter 11. The action at Heth's Salient happens, chronologically, five days before the action described in this chapter.

GPS: N 38.21124 W 77.57741

CHAPTER FIFTEEN

MAY 19, 1864

Richard Ewell surely must have been able to watch his star fall.

The Second Corps commander opened the spring campaign well enough with a solid first day in the Wilderness, but things had slowly unraveled for him since: the late start of John Gordon's flank attack on May 6, the inadvertent creation of the salient on May 8, the

breakthrough by Upton on May 10, the breakthrough by Hancock on May 12, and the sputtering tantrum he'd thrown in front of Lee that day, too. That had been a particularly personal embarrassment.

It was a puzzling turn of events for the man who had once been Stonewall Jackson's right arm. A member of West Point's Class of 1840 and a veteran of the Mexican War and the regular army, Ewell rose to prominence in the spring of 1862 when assigned to Jackson's Valley Army. Convinced his commander was crazy, Ewell soon changed his opinion when it became apparent how effectively the two worked together despite differences in temperament and leadership style.

But a wound at Second Bull Run, necessitating the amputation of his left leg below the knee, knocked him out of action until after Chancellorsville. By that time, Jackson was dead, and Lee was looking to reorganize the army. Although the commanding general didn't know Ewell well, he knew how highly Jackson had regarded him, so he elevated Ewell to command of the Second Corps hoping for the same kinds of results Jackson had delivered. Unfortunately, Ewell operated best with explicit instructions—something Lee typically didn't prescribe. Their dissimilar communication styles became a frustrating

Lt. Gen. Richard Ewell (inset)

At the site of Harris farm, a monument to the 1st Massachusetts Heavy Artillery sits on property maintained by the Central Virginia Battlefields Trust.

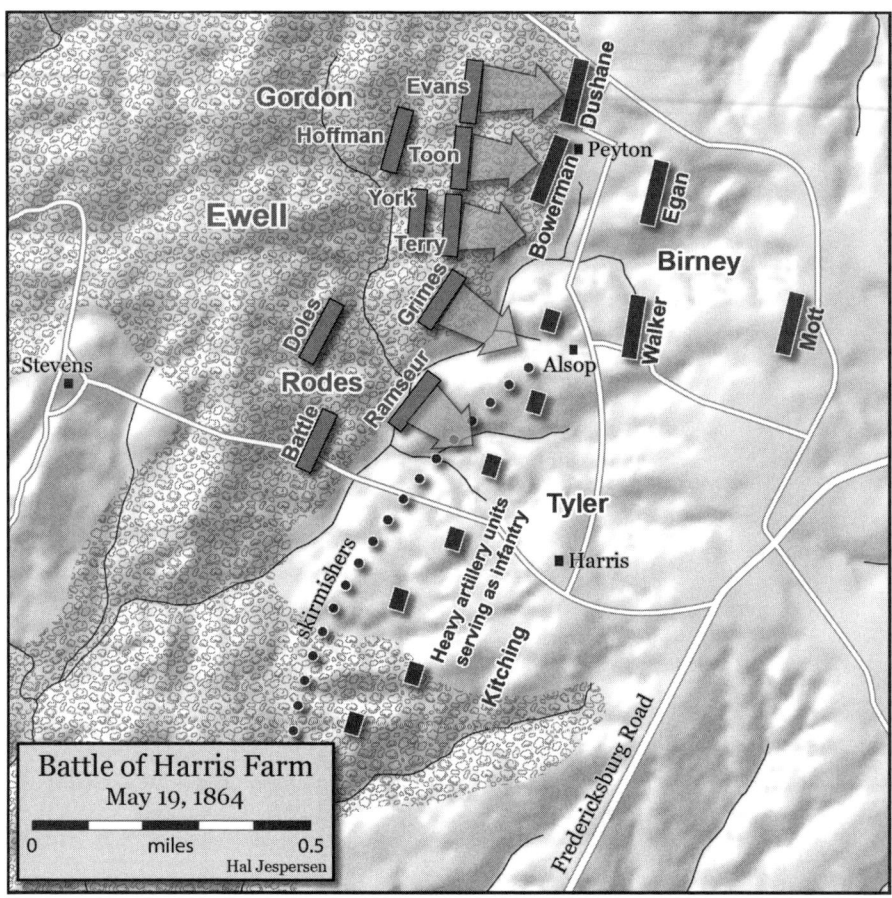

Battle of Harris Farm
May 19, 1864

0   miles   0.5

Hal Jespersen

BATTLE OF HARRIS FARM

While Confederates remained on the defensive for most of their time at Spotsylvania, Lee sent his Second Corps on a reconnaissance in force on May 19 to investigate the possibility of a strike on Grant's supply line along Fredericksburg Road. Near Harris farm, Lee's battle-hardened veterans found themselves up against green Heavy Artillery regiments new to the army. After some initial success, the Confederates quickly found themselves embroiled in combat that threatened to overwhelm them as even more fresh reinforcements to Grant's army streamed onto the battlefield for the first time and straight into the fight. Only darkness saved Lee's men.

source of disappointments for both of them, starting with the first day at Gettysburg and continuing, in ways large and small, through this latest campaign.

Not that all was bad. Even in just the last few days, Ewell had earned a few bright spots: his role in rallying the defense of Doles' Salient on the 10th, for instance, and the overwhelming victory his men had achieved on May 18.

His corps had been mauled since the start of May, though. He had, perhaps, only 6,000 effective troops, where once he'd had 15,500. From top to bottom, from major general to bedraggled private, the Second Corps stood on shaky ground.

Now Ewell found himself facing empty fields, with no Federals in sight—and orders from Lee to push out and reconnoiter the situation.

"I shall continue to strike [Grant] whenever opportunity presents itself," Lee had promised Jefferson Davis.

It was up to Ewell to find out if this was just such an opportunity.

* * *

The Second Corps had doled out such a beating to the Federal army on May 18 that Grant finally decided enough was enough. The Army of the Potomac was not going to be able to dislodge the Army of Northern Virginia.

"We found the enemy so strongly entrenched that even Grant thought it useless to knock our heads against a brick wall, and directed a suspension of the attack," Meade

The Fredericksburg Road made a more efficient and secure route of resupply and reinforcement for the Army of the Potomac.

had written to his wife that evening. "We shall now try to maneuver again, so as to draw the enemy out of his stronghold, and hope to have a fight with him before he can dig himself into an impregnable position."

So, Wright's men shifted from the extreme Federal right back to the Federal left, toward Massaponax Church Road, in preparation for a move out of Spotsylvania. Grant had decided to once more go around: left and south.

On a map, the movements of Wright's and Ewell's corps looked like the movements of a clock—the Federal VI Corps moving overnight in an arc like the small hand, with Ewell's corps moving in a wider arc, like the big hand, the following afternoon.

"[W]e stole out from our lines very secretly and marched miles to the rear of the enemy's right," wrote one of Ewell's men. Their arc took them northeast, then east, across farmlands and thick woods until they arrived along the open fields of the Harris, Alsop, and Peyton farms. The Fredericksburg Road, now being used by Federals as their main supply route, bordered the farms on the east.

The division of Maj. Gen. Robert Rodes led the Confederate advance, with trusty Brig. Gen. Stephen Ramseur—still recovering from his wound at the Bloody Angle—in the vanguard with 600 men. Before long, they stumbled into Federal pickets.

Most of the Federals came from heavy artillery units—called "heavies"—that had been stationed in the fortifications around Washington. Although trained to operate the massive siege guns there, the artillerists had also been trained as infantrymen in order to provide support for their own artillery. As Grant's army bled out during the campaign, he called the heavies in as replacements for his depleting ranks. Most of the regiments were huge, but also green.

So, when Ramseur's battle-hardened veterans stabbed into the inexperienced heavies on picket duty, the Federals crumbled. "I didn't believe there would be left ten of those greenies together in ten minutes after," a Confederate said. Only the heavies' "bulldog fighting, together with advantage of ground" saved them, observed one Federal—although the appearance of a second regiment of heavies certainly helped. That shifted the odds: 2,000 against only 600.

Ewell sent in two of John Gordon's brigades to help Ramseur, and the tide shifted again.

The heavies fell back, and some of Gordon's men even advanced as far as the Fredericksburg Road, where they intercepted a wagon train that happened to be bringing in fresh supplies. The Confederates plundered it with zeal, stalling their momentum.

More heavies arrived on the scene. For nearly all of them, it was their first battle. "[T]hey consequently went in very much jumbled up, and doubtless did fire at our own men in some few cases . . . " grumbled a Union artillerist. "Our loss was probably double what it would have been had the officers seen more service."

A mile and a half to the southeast, Grant and Meade heard the outburst. Even as they tried to figure out what in tarnation was going on, they ordered up reinforcements from the II, V, and VI corps, all stationed nearby.

As these veteran soldiers raced to the sound of the guns, the skies opened. Rain had plagued both armies since May 11, and now it returned to add more misery and confusion.

Additional reinforcements also arrived from the north, marching down from Fredericksburg to join the army. Among them was the 1st Maine Heavy Artillery regiment, which came upon the plundered supply train. "[W]e charged at the double quick, retook it, and pressed on for half or three quarters of a mile beyond," one Mainer crowed. "We kept our line under a murderous fire."

The 1st Maine Heavies were 1,800 strong and, said a veteran who then arrived on the field, "presented a splendid front to the foe—much larger than any brigade of ours . . . "

but this was their first experience on the battlefield and they didn't understand how to take advantage of the situation. Being novices in the art of war, they though it cowardly to lie down, so the Johnnies were mowing them flat. Had our arrival been delayed only a short time, they would have been nearly annihilated. The Rebel loss was insignificant; indeed I don't know that they lost any until our arrival. Being simple and cowardly enough to lie down and take advantage of the situation, we lost but two men in the time the other regiment had lost over 200. We not only took advantage of our trees and hillocks, but we dug trenches with our tin plates and bayonets.

With hundreds of experienced troops flooding onto the battlefield, Ewell again found himself under the weight of a shifting tide. Federals pushed in on all sides.

Word got back to Lee that Ewell had kicked up serious trouble, so he ordered portions of Jubal Early's Third Corps forward to link up. However, Hancock's II Corps sat squarely in front of Early's position, blocking that door.

Ewell had to sink or swim on his own.

Darkness saved him. It came early because of the rain, and it allowed Ewell to extricate his men under cover. But he left behind some 1,000 casualties—nearly 15 percent of his corps. The Federals lost as many as 1,500 men.

A few days later, Ewell fell ill. Nerves? Sick from too much time in the rain? Exhaustion? It didn't matter to Lee, who send would send Ewell to Richmond to recuperate and then use the opportunity to quietly replace him. Jubal Early, back from his temporary command of the Third Corps, would get his permanent command at the head of the Second.

At Harris Farm

The farmlands that had once belonged to Clement Harris have since been parceled into a high-end subdivision. Harris, his wife, and their three kids called their home "Bloomsbury." The farmhouse still stands, although it's a private residence, and its grounds are not open to the public.

Not far from the knoll where the Harris farm stands is a 1.7-acre parcel of land lined by cedars and owned by the Central Virginia Battlefields Trust. At the end of the parcel farthest from the road sits a stocky monument to the 1st Massachusetts Heavy Artillery, surrounded by a low iron fence. The regiment had 1,600 men on its muster roles; 25 percent of them fell as casualties during the fight at Harris farm.

Survivors of the regiment dedicated the monument on May 17, 1901, the 37th anniversary of the unit's action on the property. In the lead-up to the event, former members of the unit traveled to Petersburg, Richmond, and then Fredericksburg, where former Confederates welcomed them warmly. At Harris farm, the Bay State veterans had time to stroll the grounds prior to the dedication. At noon, the start time for the ceremony, a bugle call summoned them to assemble around the monument. It was the same bugle the company had used during the battle.

⟶ TO STOP 12

Follow Pond View Lane 0.2 miles, then turn right onto Agnes Lane, and follow it for 0.2 miles. Turn left onto Bloomsbury Lane and follow it 0.3 miles to its intersection with Route 208 and turn left. Follow Route 208 1.7 miles and, at the traffic light, bear left onto Old Court House Road. Follow Route 208 0.6 miles. At the traffic light, turn left. After 0.6 miles, bear to left onto Massaponax Church Road. Follow it 4.9 miles to Massaponax Church. Along the way, you will pass Gunnery Hill Road on the left, which leads to Myer's Hill (GPS: N 38°.19465 W 77°.56536)

GPS: N 38.19357 W 77.50977

The Campaign Moves South

CHAPTER SIXTEEN

MAY 20-21, 1864

After the failed attacks on May 18, Grant realized his time in Spotsylvania Court House was over. Lee had dug in too tightly. Confederate fortifications only got stronger over time, and interior lines let Lee easily shift men wherever and whenever he needed. Just as Grant had left behind the smoldering Wilderness, it was time to leave behind the bloody trenches. If he couldn't beat Lee out of his fortifications, Grant would maneuver him out by threatening both his supply line as well as the Confederate capital.

The general-in-chief cut orders to start the move on the evening of May 19, but Ewell's foray across Harris farm disrupted the plan. Grant passed May 20 waiting for any further shenanigans from the Confederates, but when none came, he set the Army of the Potomac into motion just after dark.

As bait, he sent Hancock's II Corps down Massaponax Road, past the church that sat at the intersection of the Telegraph Road, and then down Guiney Station Road. Along the way, Hancock met token resistance from a regiment of local Confederate cavalrymen, but he easily brushed them aside and struck onward toward Bowling Green.

Lee did not take the bait. He did, however, start pulling

Massaponax Church, modern (opposite) and historic (right)

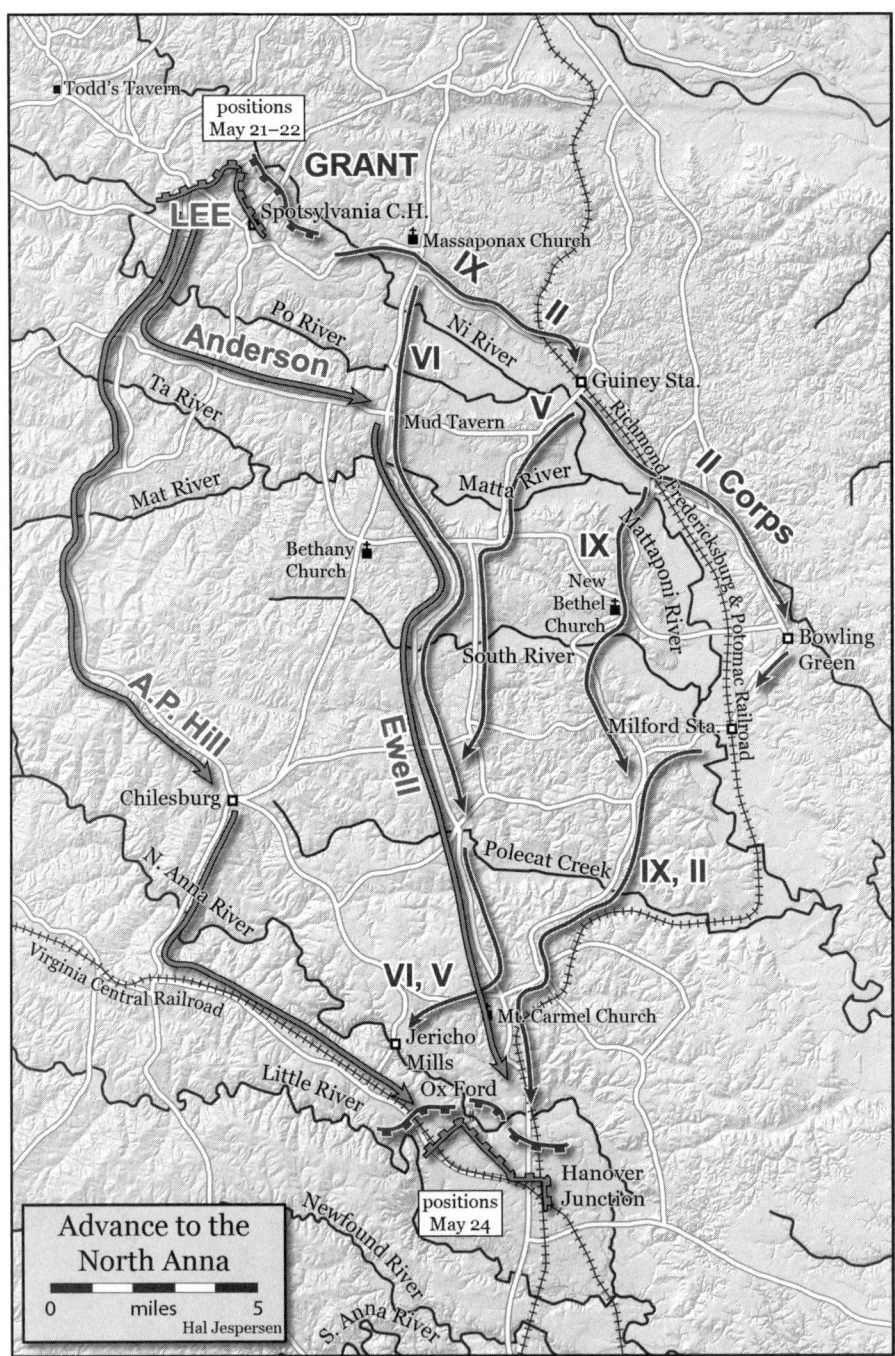

■ Todd's Tavern
positions
May 21–22
GRANT
LEE Spotsylvania C.H.
■ Massaponax Church
IX
Po River
Ni River
II
Anderson
Ta River
VI
V
Guiney Sta.
Mud Tavern
Matta River
II Corps
Mat River
Bethany Church
IX
Mattaponi River
New Bethel Church
Richmond Fredericksburg & Potomac Railroad
Ewell
South River
Polecat Creek
IX, II
Bowling Green
Milford Sta.
A.P. Hill
Chilesburg □
N. Anna River
Virginia Central Railroad
VI, V
Mt. Carmel Church
Jericho Mills
Little River
Ox Ford
Hanover Junction
positions May 24
Newfound River
S. Anna River

Advance to the
North Anna

0   miles   5
Hal Jespersen

ADVANCE TO THE NORTH ANNA—Grant tried to lure Lee out of the Confederate position around Spotsylvania by dangling Hancock's II Corps as bait off to the southeast near Bowling Green. The wily Lee declined to fall for it, instead marching south to take up a physically dominating position along the south bank of the North Anna River. Recognizing how vulnerable his own divided army then was, Grant rushed to reunite it and, in turn, nearly stumbled into a trap set by Lee. Lee maintained the tactical advantage but, with his back so close to Richmond, lost crucial room to maneuver.

Grant, with his back to the camera, leans over a church pew to consult with Meade, seated.

off the Spotsylvania Court House Line. He ordered Ewell to assume a position south of the Po River to block Grant's most direct route to Richmond along the Telegraph Road, which also allowed Lee to hold the inside track to the capital. Third Corps, now back under the command of Lt. Gen. A. P. Hill, withdrew shortly thereafter.

Grant and Meade continued pulling men off the line, as well. Warren's corps was ordered to follow Hancock. Burnside's corps hit the road, as well, marching on a route more directly south along the Telegraph Road—only to be stymied by Ewell's unexpected appearance as a roadblock.

On the morning of May 21, Grant and Meade stopped along the traffic-choked Telegraph Road at the Massaponax Church. Staffers pulled pews out into the front yard and set them in a wide circle. The commanders studied their maps and conferred with their officers, the hubbub of headquarters swirling all around them: men carrying papers, holding horses, talking about the march, the campaigns, their news from home.

Photographer Timothy O'Sullivan climbed into the uppermost cranny of the church and pointed his camera out the east window. He snapped three pictures. They are the only three known photographs of this council of war. Much of the activity shows up only as blurs.

These excellent photographs all but mark the end of the battle of Spotsylvania Court House.

The race to the North Anna River was on.

Timothy O'Sullivan

* * *

"There is no enthusiasm in the army for Gen. Grant," a colonel from Maine had said of the new general-in-chief shortly after Grant's appointment; "and, on the other hand, there is no prejudice against him. We are prepared to throw up our hats for him when he shows himself the great soldier here in Virginia against Lee and the best troops of the rebels." Indeed, it had seemed that Lee would serve as the great litmus test. "Grant has never met Bobby Lee yet," Federals said.

By May 21, the Overland campaign was 17 days old. Grant had met Bobby Lee and shown what kind of soldier he was.

"Grant turns Lee's flank"

Just as importantly, Grant had learned much about the Army of the Potomac. It was a far more political beast than he was used to. In action, it moved with a strange kind of inaction, a cumbersome slowness that stymied its own potential for success.

Grant had initially taken a hands-off approach with its operations, satisfied to let Meade handle the reigns, but as the campaign wore on, Grant became more actively involved.

As a result, it's difficult to assess Meade's performance. On the evening of May 7, he was still fully in control of his army. He kicked the cavalry from bed, as he should have, in an attempt to open the way to Spotsylvania Court House, and he allowed Warren to have the latitude he needed in attack at Laurel Hill that first day—but then faltered by not taking control at the front as he should have. Nor did he order Sedgwick to assume command at the front to coordinate the combined assault of the V and VI corps.

By May 10, Grant was calling most of the shots. Meade, as a consequence, took on a role more like that of a staff officer than an army commander.

Among the army's corps commanders, Hancock clearly stood out as the best. To that end, Grant would make the II Corps a victim of its own success, using it as his sledgehammer, which would cost the corps lives and experienced officers.

At the other extreme, Warren had demonstrated oddly erratic behavior: temerity and timidity that combined aggressiveness with passive-aggressiveness. Where once Grant had looked at Warren as a possible replacement for Meade should anything happen to the army commander, he now realized what a terrible mistake that would have made. Warren's star had fallen so low that Grant and Meade almost relieved him of command on May 12—an action that would have been entirely justified.

Ambrose Burnside, although more experienced than any of the others, lacked the killer instinct needed to win a battle. He had lost any fighting edge he once possessed. The unwieldy structure of his independent command was proving to be a costly distraction, too; by the time of the next battle, the IX Corps would again be folded back into the Army of the Potomac. Even that would not compensate for Burnside's spectacular mediocrity as a field commander, though.

For all Sedgwick's slowness, Grant missed his experience. "His loss to this army is greater than the loss of a whole division of troops," he'd said. His replacement, Horatio Wright, still represented a question mark, although Grant was starting to like what he saw. Wright's drinking on May 12 may have cost him some nerve—and cost men their lives—but he started to work his corps with the precision of a veteran commander by the end of the third week of May.

The only other major star to emerge from the campaign, aside from Hancock, was Phil Sheridan—but that had far more to do with Grant's esteem for him than anything else. Sheridan's cavalry failed to catch the Confederate approach to the Wilderness and then failed to clear the road to Spotsylvania. Grant let Sheridan's confrontation with Meade weaken Meade's position as army commander, and Sheridan's departure hamstrung the Army of the Potomac without eyes and ears at a time when the army desperately needed cavalry. Finally, Sheridan's ride to Richmond was a sloppy affair that accomplished little. However, because the confrontation at Yellow Tavern ended in Jeb Stuart's death, Sheridan apparently got a free pass on everything else.

Then there was Grant himself. The "dust-covered man," as he'd been called, contended as much with mud as with Confederates. Time and again, he looked for the opportunity to out-maneuver Lee, but the increasingly wet weather worked against him. He expected troops to march over muddy, dark roads, from one end of the line to the other, for dawn attacks. Even under the best circumstances, such marches would have been nearly impossible; considering the conditions, Grant's expectations were unreasonable.

Grant's critics have been quick to label the general "Grant the Butcher"—someone who ordered troops to mindlessly throw themselves in frontal assaults against strong fortifications. Such criticism ignores Grant's willingness to listen to officers like Emory Upton, who offered new innovations. It also ignores Grant's ability to learn on the fly, such as the way his attack plan for May 12 built on the successes of Upton's attack on May 10. Finally, it ignores the chess-like way Grant maneuvered troops

Grant moves south

across the countryside in an attempt to force checkmate. While Grant did resort at times to frontal assaults, it was but one type of many tools he used.

Grant knew from the beginning that the conflict would ultimately come down to numbers. He didn't grind down the Army of Northern Virginia because he wasn't creative enough to do anything else; he did it because he alone had the resolve to do what the grim arithmetic of war demanded.

"We have found Grant a tough old customer but have no idea of letting him whip us," said a Confederate artillerist. "It is reported that he is being rapidly reinforced but we can kill them as fast as they come."

Grim arithmetic, indeed.

*   *   *

Robert E. Lee and his army had been roughly handled—battered, but not broken. Although on the defensive for almost all of the campaign, he continued to look at ways to grab the initiative and strike a blow.

Of critical concern were the losses he'd suffered in his command structure. On a personal level, he felt the loss of Jeb Stuart most keenly. "He never brought me a piece of false information," Lee said when he heard the news, just before retiring to his tent to weep. He looked at Stuart very much like one of his own sons. Fortunately for the army, Lee had other highly capable cavalry commanders who could fill the void Stuart left, so Stuart's death was not the crippling blow Sheridan wanted everyone to believe it was.

Of equal concern on the battlefield was the loss of his second-in-command, James Longstreet, in the Wilderness. Fortunately, the new First Corps commander, Richard Anderson, did a fine job in his first battle as a corps commander. He made critical decisions at critical times, thus blocking the Federal approach to the Court House.

Third Corps also performed well under new leadership. Lee missed the experience of A. P. Hill, who was back in the saddle by the time the army moved out of Spotsylvania, but Hill's temporary replacement, Jubal Early, had performed with distinction. Early was an irascible bundle of energy who skillfully deployed his corps both on the offensive and defensive. Lee could have asked little more out of either Early or Anderson.

But the question of Richard Ewell hung in the air like the brewing rainclouds. Ewell fought a nearly flawless defensive battle in the Wilderness and showed signs of brilliance in his counterattacks at Doles' Salient on May 10, but he outright cracked under pressure in front of Lee and his men on May 12 and he nearly led his corps to total destruction at Harris farm on May 19. Lee's confidence in Ewell had been shaken irreparably.

Not that Lee was blameless. His engineer's eye had doubted the Mule Shoe's security, but he let the line stand. When it fell, Lee was as much to blame as anyone because he had ordered the withdrawal of the very artillery necessary to make the formation defensible and then didn't bother to tell his subordinates on the field. In the end, the decision cost him 22 cannon, more than 3,000 desperately needed men, and two veteran generals.

Confederate prisoners

Overall, Lee's losses at Spotsylvania numbered between 10,000 and 12,000 men, including nearly an entire division captured. Fortunately for him, reinforcements from Richmond, Petersburg, and the Shenandoah were on the way to bolster the army. What he gained in reinforcements, though, he lost in ground as Grant and Meade crept closer to Richmond.

For the Union army, the cost of Spotsylvania Court House had been even higher: nearly 18,000 Union casualties. In all, more than 36,000 Federals had become casualties since the campaign opened. Like Lee, Grant received reinforcements, too. Where Lee's were veteran fighters, though, Grant's were bandbox soldiers who'd yet to see the elephant. Many had seen more time in the bar rooms and brothels of Washington than time on the battlefield. What Grant made up for in numbers, he more than lacked in combat-experienced officers and men.

*   *   *

The grapple between Grant and Lee would continue for nearly a month longer: along the banks of the North Anna River and then Totopotomoy Creek, across the fields of Cold Harbor, and finally over the James River to the outskirts of Petersburg. There, the running battle would settle into a siege that would stretch on from mid-June through a stifling sticky summer, an anxious autumn, and a bitter, bitter winter, all the way until April.

By then, Appomattox would be only days away.

The Battle of Yellow Tavern

APPENDIX A
BY DANIEL T. DAVIS

Major General Philip Sheridan was blistering with anger as he stormed toward the headquarters of George Meade, the commander of the Army of the Potomac. This confrontation was a long time in the making. Sheridan, the commander of the army's cavalry corps, and Meade had been at loggerheads over the proper use of cavalry since their first meeting. However, it was the failings of the last day and a half that were foremost in Sheridan's mind.

After a two-day stalemate in the Wilderness, General-in-Chief Ulysses S. Grant had elected to move Meade's Potomac Army around the Confederate right flank to Spotsylvania Court House. The key piece in this operation was to secure the Brock Road, the main thoroughfare that ran from the Wilderness to Spotsylvania. If the Federals wished to arrive at the critical crossroads ahead of the Confederates, they would have wrest control of it from Maj. Gen. J. E. B. Stuart's horsemen. This task fell to Sheridan. Throughout May 7, the Union cavalry attempted fruitlessly to clear the road from its staunch defenders. The failure on the part of Sheridan forced Meade to bypass him early on the morning of May 8 and issue orders directly to Sheridan's subordinates. More importantly, the delaying action executed by Stuart allowed the Confederate infantry to outpace their counterparts and arrive at Spotsylvania ahead of the Yankees. As in the Wilderness, the Union advance had been stymied. Recognizing the catastrophe, Sheridan resolved that he would not be made a scapegoat and went to confront Meade.

Sheridan lit into Meade, accusing him of overreaching his authority by becoming too involved in the matters of his cavalry. Meade was widely known for his fiery temper and was not going to take Sheridan lightly. One witness said that Meade fired back "hammer and tongs" and blamed Sheridan for the delays the army had sustained as they moved out of the Wilderness. The air filled with epithets

Not much remains of the Yellow Tavern battlefield. Except for a monument commemorating Stuart's wounding, the battlefield has been swallowed by suburban sprawl. The memorial stands very close to the spot where Stuart fell. "He was fearless and faithful," the monument opines, "pure and powerful, tender and true."

General Philip Sheridan and several of his subordinates. Sheridan stands in the center, third from left. Pictured are, from left to right, Henry Davies, David M. Gregg, Sheridan, Wesley Merrit, Alfred Torbert, and James Wilson. All of the men, except Torbert, would participate in the Yellow Tavern operations.

as the skirmish reached a crescendo. Scorched with rage, Sheridan finally exclaimed that he could single-handedly whip Stuart and his cavalry if Meade would only give him the opportunity. With that, Sheridan stalked off. Meade immediately set out to report the incident to Grant. Upon hearing of Sheridan's boast, Grant replied, "Did Sheridan say that? Well, he generally knows what he is talking about. Let him start right out and do it." Within the hour, Meade's chief-of-staff was drafting orders directing Sheridan to prepare an offensive against Stuart's cavalry.

That afternoon, Sheridan assembled his troopers at his headquarters near the old Chancellorsville battlefield. Briefing his three division commanders—Wesley Merritt, David Gregg, and James Wilson— of his plans, Sheridan proposed to give Stuart a "fair, square fight." Preparations were made throughout the remainder of the day as Sheridan charted the route he and his men would take. The entire cavalry corps, all 10,000 troopers, would set out in an attempt to bring the vaunted Stuart to battle. Although this was a tremendous undertaking, it would effectively deprive the Army of the Potomac of its eyes and ears for the remainder of the fighting at Spotsylvania.

On the morning of May 9, Sheridan led his three divisions out of their encampment and headed east. His goal was to swing well around the armies engaged in Spotsylvania, drawing Stuart after him in the process. The decisive battle Sheridan was hoping for would occur somewhere to the south, between Spotsylvania and the Confederate capital at Richmond. The Union horsemen were strung out for miles; witnesses remembered it took around four hours for the column to pass a certain point. Reaching the Telegraph Road near Fredericksburg, the troopers turned south. The march continued past Massaponax Church and on toward Mud Tavern. Hoping that the fish would take the worm, Sheridan headed the column to the southwest as he approached the North Anna River, and the Yankees rode toward Beaver Dam.

The fish was indeed taking the bait. Stuart had begun receiving reports of the Union movement that morning and sent one of his brigades, under the command of Brig. Gen. Williams C. Wickham, to trail the column. Stuart himself would leave Spotsylvania that afternoon to overtake Fitzhugh Lee who followed in Wickham's wake. Wickham, meanwhile, would spend the better part of the day skirmishing along the Telegraph Road with Sheridan's rearguard, commanded by the capable Brig. Gen. Henry Davies. The Gray Cavalier would also call on the brigades of Brig. Gen. Lunsford Lomax and James Gordon to join Wickham as he continued his pursuit of Sheridan.

Despite the harassment of Wickham's troopers in his rear, Sheridan was making good time and by nightfall reached Anderson's Ford on the North Anna. While most of the corps remained on the opposite bank, Brig. Gen. George A. Custer's Michiganders, supported by elements of Brig. Gen. Thomas Devin's brigade, crossed the river and rode toward Beaver Dam Station on the Virginia Central Railroad. There, Custer and his men freed a contingent of Union soldiers bound for Southern prison camps and destroyed two trains and a number of valuable supplies before putting the station and surrounding buildings to the torch. The Yankees bedded down that evening beneath the flames of Beaver Dam.

The next morning, the Federal horsemen set out once again. The head start they had gained on the Confederates the previous day was paying dividends, no matter how slight the start was. Stuart had planned to cross a force upstream from Anderson's Ford on May 10 to attack the head of the Union column while simultaneously keeping up pressure on Sheridan's rear. Due to the distance traveled and the condition of his men and horses by the time Stuart arrived on the banks of the North Anna, Sheridan was gone. This left him to cast about for other options in attacking the Yankee column. It seemed that Sheridan was angling toward Richmond. After some deliberation, Stuart decided that his best hope would be to assail the Northerners somewhere around the Confederate capital. This plan entailed an extremely tiring march around Sheridan, but

Stuart and his cavalry

to Stuart it was his best chance for success.

Meanwhile, the Union advance continued. Brigadier General Wesley Merritt remembered that "the day was very hot and the march…was made with but little water or rest for our animals." By late afternoon, they reached Ground Squirrel Bridge on the South Anna River, having traveled nearly 20 miles from Beaver Dam Station. After crossing, the bridge was destroyed in order to deter any enemy pursuit. Then, the Federals went into camp for the night.

Reveille sounded before sunrise the next morning. In Sheridan's mind, the battle he had been waiting and hoping for would have to take place sometime that day. His men had ridden hard for two days with Rebel horsemen nipping at the rear of the column. Although no significant force had been encountered, the Union horsemen were quickly approaching the outer defenses of Richmond. The blue troopers were about to force Stuart's hand and he would have to act. Thus, Sheridan directed Merritt to take the lead in the line of march, to be followed closely by Wilson. The column would head east along the Mountain Road and in the direction of the Rebel capital.

The Beau Sabreur had ably completed his round about ride. Stopping briefly at Taylorsville on the night of May 10, he continued on toward Ashland and the Telegraph Road. The road had played a significant role for Sheridan during the early stages of the operation. It would be just as important for Stuart during the latter stages.

From Ashland, Telegraph Road continued south before intersecting with the Brook Turnpike above Richmond. The Mountain Road, the main route on which Sheridan was operating, joined with the Brook Turnpike near its intersection with the Telegraph Road. Stuart planned to advance south along the Telegraph Road to where these roads intersected and intercept Sheridan. Around 8 o'clock on the morning of May 11, the first of Stuart's brigades, under Lunsford Lomax, began taking up a position along the Telegraph Road above the intersection of the Mountain Road and Brook Turnpike. Lomax's men dismounted and deployed, facing toward the west around an old hostelry known as Yellow Tavern.

It was not more than an hour after Lomax completed his dispositions that the Union cavalry arrived. Seeing the Rebels deployed, Sheridan sent orders to Wesley Merritt to dismount his brigades and move against the Confederate line. Merritt's first division, Custer's Wolverines, moved against Lomax's right but immediately ran into stubborn opposition. With Custer's advance ground to a halt, the brigades of Thomas Devin and Col. Alfred Gibbs surged forward on Custer's right. The added weight of Devin and Gibbs was enough to force the Rebels to withdraw. One Federal trooper remembered that the Confederates "broke and ran like a flock of sheep." Lomax's men did run, northward to high ground along the Telegraph Road.

Sheridan watched as his men had driven Lomax away from his position around Yellow Tavern. Now, the Confederates could be seen rallying on a ridge just to the north. There, Stuart reformed his men. Wickham's brigade, which had begun arriving just as the fighting commenced, formed the right of the line along the ridge. Lomax's disheartened troopers fell in on Wickham's left. Between the two brigades, Stuart placed the Baltimore Light Artillery in the center of his line.

Not willing to settle with just brushing aside a lone Rebel brigade, Sheridan determined to attack Stuart's new line. As Stuart received the reinforcement of Wickham's brigade, Sheridan would use the added weight of James Wilson's division to support the upcoming assault. Leading the main assault would be the young George Custer, who was quickly becoming one of Sheridan's most reliable subordinates. Custer elected to concentrate his efforts on the artillery in the center of the Confederate line. Custer would send the 5th and 6th Michigan in on his left, while the 1st and 7th Michigan, supported by the 1st Vermont, would assault the Maryland artillery. Wilson would support Custer's left while Gibbs would support his right.

The Union cavalry moved out around four o'clock. Moving rapidly, the Yankees ascended the ridge under fire and pushed toward the enemy lines. Recognizing the threat to his guns, Stuart called for support from the veteran 1st

"Unhorsed trooper returns from Sheridan's raid."

Opposite: Stuart's grave at Hollywood Cemetery in Richmond, Virginia

Virginia Cavalry. The men from the Commonwealth arrived just in time to meet the Northerners. However, the ongoing pressure offered by the 1st Vermont and the 7th Michigan was too much to withstand and the Confederate line collapsed. The men from Wickham's and Lomax's brigades scattered and ran as Union troopers occupied the ridge.

One Confederate in particular would not make it off the ridge that day. Stuart had remained near his artillery throughout the assault. It was here an enemy cavalryman spotted him. Probably not knowing who his target was, the Federal trooper took careful aim and fired. The bullet struck Stuart in the abdomen. Despite the situation on the ridge, his men were able to get Stuart into an ambulance. Traveling through an evening thunderstorm, the ambulance and small cavalcade of staff officers reached Richmond. There, in a house on West Grace Street, Stuart passed away just after 7:30 p.m. on May 12, 1864.

The reverberations could be felt shortly after the smoke of the battle had blown away. The Confederacy lost one of its premier officers at a time when superb leadership was at a premium. Stuart's eventual replacement, Maj. Gen. Wade Hampton, would prove up to the task of handling Lee's cavalry. In June, the South Carolinian would defeat Sheridan at the battle of Trevilian Station and would remain a burr under the saddle of his enemies for months to come.

At the same time, the relationship between Philip Sheridan and George Meade was irreparable. The two would be unable to work together harmoniously for the remainder of the war.

The greatest impact, though, may have been with the troopers in the cavalry corps of the Army of the Potomac. Taken as a whole, the victory and mortal wounding of Stuart became a symbol of pride for the Yankees. This object of motivation would prove crucial to their morale in the battles yet to come.

Civilians on the Battlefield

APPENDIX B
BY KATHLEEN LOGOTHETIS

Sarah Spindle and Family

Sarah Spindle lived in this home as household head with five children and young adults, plus 18 slaves. She owned 312 acres of land valued at $3,000 and $14,600 worth of personal property. The house itself was a wooden two-and-a-half-story building with an orchard and outbuilding nearby. On May 8, 1864, the opening stages of the battle of Spotsylvania swirled around the Spindle home. The battle of Laurel Hill resulted in the destruction of the family home. "It is said that this building was set on fire by an exploding shell while the family was inside at breakfast," a New York soldier said. The Spindles never rebuilt and presumably relocated elsewhere. The site of the Spindle house ruins is located on the Laurel Hill section of the battlefield and can be accessed using the self-guided walking trail.

The farm lane that leads to the site where the Spindle house once stood

Edgar and Ann Harrison

Edgar and Ann Harrison lived in their home named "La Villa" with three children, all under the age of six, and 11 slaves. Their one-and-a-half-story wooden home was situated on 190 acres of land between Brock and Gordon Roads. Edgar served in Company E, 9th Virginia Cavalry during the war, leaving Ann home with the children and slaves. Early in the battle, the family escaped to the rear as the bullets started flying. A slave sent back to the property later reported that the livestock was gone, the slave quarters had been pulled down to build the breastworks, and the yard was full of graves. After the war, the building fell into disrepair and burned down. The Harrison house site is off Gordon Road and can be accessed using the self-guided walking trail.

The Harrison house

Opposite: The site of the former Landrum house

147

Neil McCoull and family

Woodshaw farm, the home of Neil McCoull and the three women living with him, became the center

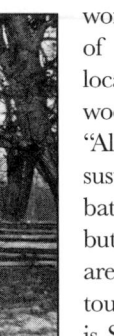

of the Confederate lines at Spotsylvania, located in the center of the Muleshoe. The wooden structure served as Maj. Gen. Edward "Allegheny" Johnson's headquarters and sustained considerable damage during the battle. After the war, the building was repaired, but burned down in 1921. Only the foundations are visible today as a stop on the NPS driving tour of the battlefield. The McCoull house site is Stop #5 on the Park Service's Spotsylvania Battlefield driving tour.

The McCoull house

The Landrum Family

The four-room Landrum house was home to Willis Landrum and six other people, four of them children

under the age of 12. Their 170-acres farm served as a starting point for the Union army's attack on May 12, 1864, against the Confederate line—the action known as the Bloody Angle. In 1939, Lucy Landrum, the youngest of the inhabitants, shared that her family had been warned of the upcoming action the night before and were hurried out of the area during the afternoon of May 12. The home was destroyed during the campaign, but the Landrums returned and rebuilt on the site of the original house. This

Historic view of the Landrum farm fields

second structure was destroyed by fire in 1897.

The Landrum house ruins are located a couple hundred yards from the Bloody Angle stop on the driving tour and can be accessed from the self-guided walking trail.

The Brown Farm

The Union II Corps arrayed itself for its May 12 attack

in the fields of 77-year-old John C. Brown, who lived on his 1,772-acres farm with his wife, Elizabeth, six other family members who ranged in age from 3 to 33 years old, and 43 slaves. Their farmhouse was one and a half stories tall and included at least four outbuildings. Brown's son, James—who also lived at the house—served in the 9th Virginia Cavalry, but was discharged due to dyspepsia

A sketch of the Brown farm with the II Corps assembling for battle

in July 1862; he was conscripted later into the 30th Virginia Infantry and later captured at Hatcher's Run on April 3, 1865 and sent to Point Lookout Prison.

Clement and Mary Harris

Clement and Mary Harris lived with their three young children and 16 slaves at "Bloomsbury" about 2.5 miles northwest of Spotsylvania Court House. On May 19, 1864, the last major engagement of the battle of Spotsylvania, known as the battle of Harris Farm, swirled through the fields of Bloomsbury, which was already being used as a field hospital. The family took refuge in the basement and both they and the structure survived the battle. Sadly, Clement Harris died a few years later in 1867, "not having recovered from the horrors of war." The house still stands and is a private residence. The Harris house is a privately owned residence located off Route 208 about 500 yards southwest of the intersection of Routes 208 and 628.

Bloomsbury

The Spotsylvania Courthouse

The namesake of the town and the battle that would surround it was a one-and-a-half story brick courthouse located at the intersection of the Brock and Court House roads. The courthouse yard was enclosed by a low brick wall with a jailhouse, tavern, two churches, and several private residences nearby; these were collectively known as "Spotsylvania Court House." The courthouse of 1864 was the third build by the county, and it would not be the last. The building sustained considerable damage (as did the county records) from the battle, and although it was repaired and reoccupied by the county government after the war, eventually they deemed it structurally unsafe. It was torn down in 1901, and the county erected a new courthouse in a similar design on the same site.

The Spotsylvania Courthouse

The courthouse (in photo, left) with the Spotsylvania Hotel at the head of the street (in photo, right). The Spotsylvania Hotel was also known as the Sanford Hotel.

A History of the Battlefield

APPENDIX C
BY JOHN F. CUMMINGS III

When the armies left Spotsylvania Court House on May 21, 1864, after two weeks of virtual stalemate, they left behind a wrecked landscape and an impoverished civilian population. The beleaguered populace felt abandoned to fend for itself on farms laid barren and stripped of sustenance after nearly two years of imposition by friend and foe. The slave population that had made up virtually half of the county's antebellum numbers was mostly gone, enjoying an exodus to freedom. Now, many of the remaining white citizens were about to call it quits.

Northern journalist John Trowbridge visited Spotsylvania the summer after the war and recorded his impressions of the destitute people and the wreckage of war still cast about. Amongst miles of abandoned earthworks and discarded equipage lay barely covered human remains, their bleached bones still clad in their uniforms and shoes. The southern dead remained as they had fallen. Near the infamous Bloody Angle, Trowbridge noted what appeared to be women and children gathering nuts along the forest floor, only to find out upon closer inspection that they were collecting thousands of fired bullets to sell for scrap. Living was reduced to desperation. At the Courthouse proper, the clerk of the court recovered volumes of county records that had been buried nearby for safety, prior to the fighting. The building had suffered such severe structural damage that by 1900 it required extensive shoring up.

With the turn of the century, Spotsylvania had a population of little more than 9,000 across its roughly 400 square miles. Of that, most folks lived along the eastern extent of its borders, closest to the main north-to-south transportation corridors and nestled in close to the city of Fredericksburg. Nine miles as the crow flies below the city, at the Bloody Angle, three monuments had been erected by

Graves on the Spotsylvania battlefield were marked with simple planks. Bodies were later reinterred in the Confederate cemetery near the Court House.

Opposite: The only remaining structure from the C.C.C. camp is now used as an NPS maintenance facility.

151

Veterans revisit the Spostylvania battlefield.

veterans' groups of Northern regiments that had suffered the campaign. These stood on small, fenced parcels inside farm fields actively cultivated by the Landrum family. The Landrums had witnessed the fighting that played out on their property, sheltered beneath their modest dwelling; they endured the battle, rebuilt their farm, and survived on the land. Efforts by several local and national veterans' groups to establish a military park in the region failed to gain Congressional support.

In the 1920s, the War Department took a renewed interest in the rural battlefields in Spotsylvania County with the intent of bringing a military park to reality. Officially named "Fredericksburg and Spotsylvania County Battlefields Memorial National Military Park," it was established on Valentine's Day in 1927 and dedicated a year later by President Calvin Coolidge during a ceremony held at the Fredericksburg Country Club. Land acquisition was brisk until the Great Depression brought work to a standstill.

As a byproduct of recovery efforts to end the Depression, President Franklin Roosevelt established the Civilian Conservation Corps (C.C.C.) in 1933. In June of that year, the first of Spotsylvania County's four C.C.C. camps opened near the site of the former McCoull house at the center of the Mule Shoe. MP-1, as it was called, employed mostly WWI veterans—skilled tradesmen and craftsmen—rather than the late-teen/early-twentyish young men who typically made up a C.C.C. encampment. "Our armies must become peace armies," said C.C.C. Director Robert Fechner, speaking at a 1933 Remembrance Day ceremony at the Spotsylvania camp, "engaged in constructive work, repairing damage to our natural resources and making this country healthier, better, lovelier, and more productive for those who are to come."

MP-1 operated through April 1936. The efforts of those men built the infrastructure of the park, including the all-important road system that allowed tourists easy interior access to the former farm fields. Workers also improved deteriorating earthworks by shoring them up with more dirt, constructed a set of reproduction earthworks near the Bloody Angle, and performed widespread tree surgery. They also cleared ditches and reduced fire hazards. The many improvements to the park provided a boost to the regional economy.

One private benefactor also played an important role in the battlefield's preservation at this time. Battlefield enthusiast Edward T. Stuart, a Philadelphia philanthropist, owned 32 acres of core battlefield property at the Bloody Angle. Just prior to his death in 1940, Stuart donated his holdings to the Military Order of the Loyal Legion of the

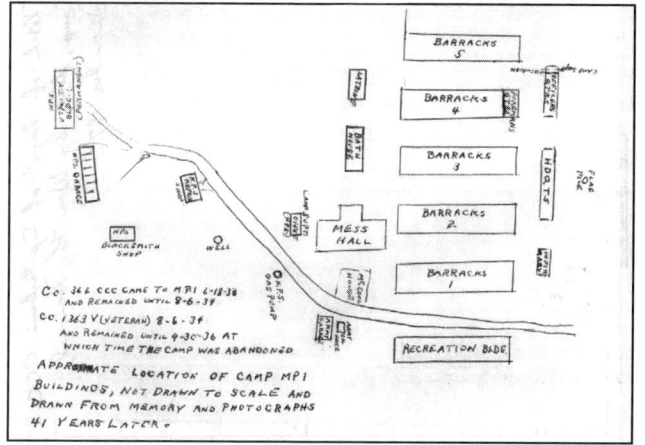

A sketch of the groundplan of the Spotsy C.C.C. camp

United States (MOLLUS), which then added another 130 acres to the parcel and donated it to the NPS. Stuart was the son of George H. Stuart, who headed the United States Christian Commission during the Civil War.

As the Civil War Centennial approached, the park underwent another series of improvements thanks to "Mission 66," a program designed to improve visitor experiences and celebrate the 50th anniversary of the National Park Service in 1966. New Visitor Centers and interpretive shelters replaced the rustic "contact stations" the C.C.C. had built in the 1930s.

Spotsylvania County was for many years a seemingly remote, rural location where most imagined the land would stay largely undeveloped and true to its historic nature. The late 20th century, however, ushered in unprecedented growth as the region became an extension of the Washington, D.C. suburbs. Encroachment was countered by several Herculean efforts to protect threatened sites throughout the county. Initially a vastly spread 2,100 acres, the park now exceeds 8,400. Just under 1,500 of those acres are at Spotsylvania Court House.

The core of the Spotsylvania Battlefield is considered to be the crown jewel of the park by many because of its pristine nature, and is largely protected from visual encroachment. Visitors can appreciate unobstructed terrain in much the same way the soldiers saw it. Sections of the paved road within the park, initially designed to permit automobile traffic to drive within the entire Mule Shoe Salient, were removed around the turn of the century to create a more pedestrian experience. Fifty years after the Civil War Centennial, the Spotsylvania Battlefield underwent an extensive revitalization to its interpretive offerings with many new wayside markers; landscape restoration around the Bloody Angle; and new walking paths.

Spotsylvania in Memory
APPENDIX D
BY CHRIS MACKOWSKI

We cross the last hundred yards of open field that the Union soldiers could not cross—from the paved park road that runs parallel to "Lee's Second Line" toward the Harrison house. Our path runs through patches of grasses, ferns, and scrub watercolored with the first brushes of emerging fall color. We pass over the trickle of a stream before hiking up the final rise to the house site itself. No Union soldier made it this far, even with the protection offered by the hill.

I have come with a friend to Spotsylvania, to what had once been the interior of the Mule Shoe Salient, to find one of the battlefield's forgotten stories. The Federal assaults on May 18, 1864, stand as a testament to the power of engineering over infantry in one of the most futile efforts of Grant's entire Overland Campaign.

But to look at the field today, there's nary an indication that anything happened here at all.

The Federal assault on May 18 deserves attention because it was just as large as the Federal assault against the Mule Shoe on May 12. It covered the same ground and used the same tactics, and it pitted many of the same Federals against the same Confederates. Yet the outcome could not have been more different.

Ewell's veterans, so bruised on May 12, had spent the intervening six days doing nothing but resting and fortifying. The works they created were the strongest field fortifications seen in the Eastern Theater to date.

The remnants of those works still wind along the crest of the hill through the woods along the Spotsylvania history trail. They are among the best-preserved earthworks accessible to visitors in the park.

In front of the works, Confederates had spread "acres of abatis" and a picket line. "As the Confederate skirmishers were swept back before the strong lines of blue," wrote one Massachusetts soldier, "the restrained tempest broke forth, and with shriek and scream and hissing, poured its death blast in the faces of the Union soldiers."

The Confederate artillery "mowed the men down in

rows," wrote a Rhode Islander. One Confederate called it "terrible execution."

The smoke and cacophony of battle "filled the valleys, and rested on the hills of all this wilderness, hung in lurid haze all around the horizon, and built a dense canopy overhead," wrote a Union medical officer—so different than this quiet overcast evening when my friend and I walk the ground.

"For a few minutes all was observed in mystery," said Maj. Wesley Brainerd of the 50th New York Engineers. "Moments seemed like hours . . . Soon the smoke cleared away and disclosed the ground for long distances thickly strewn with our dead and dying men. It was an awfully grand spectacle, one often repeated around that ground which has been justly styled 'Bloody Spotsylvania.'"

Federal casualties on the field totaled some 1,250 men. Most of them were "torn all to pieces with canon balls," said one Confederate observer. A Richmond newspaper explained that "[v]ery little musketry was used in this engagement, for the reason that the enemy did not come near enough our lines."

I stand at the crest of the hill and look back across the assault field and really think about that: Confederate artillery laid down such devastating fire that Confederate infantry hardly had to engage. What must it have been like out there on that field, all patchwork color this evening but all blue and blood and smoky gray on that May morning years ago?

No traces of the carnage remain on the field, of course—but no traces remain in the public imagination or memory, either. The only interpretive marker on this part of the battlefield sits on a small plot of grass near the ruins of the Harrison house, where Lee and Ewell made their headquarters before the May 12 assault. The sign, which is decades old, explains the site's significance to that incident, but it remains mute on the May 18 attack. It remains mute on the Harrison family, too.

That surprises me a little considering the emphasis in recent years on slave and civilian stories. Despite the public's continued interest, military history has become untrendy among most academics and scholars. Much of this battlefield's military history remains untold and unexplored.

That's true of the battle of Spotsylvania Court House in general, too. It generally gets no attention of its own but instead gets grouped in as part of Grant's Overland campaign, which seldom makes the list of anyone's favorite battles. I hear Gettysburg and Antietam or "Lee's Greatest Victory" at Chancellorsville. Shiloh pops up now and then. First Manassas. If the Overland campaign gets mentioned at all, it's usually because of the dark mystique of the Wilderness or because of Cold Harbor and Grant's infamous June 3 attack there, where he lost as many as 7,000 men in 15 minutes.

The Bloody Angle sometimes gets mentioned. After all, it has one of those irresistibly sensationalized names that attracts so much attention, like its cousins the Bloody Pond at Shiloh and the Bloody Lane at Antietam. Civil War veterans had a flair for the melodramatic when it came to catchy names. I think of the Slaughter Pen, the Devil's Den, the Battle Above the Clouds. Say "The Cornfield" to any Civil War buff and that person will nod grimly and knowingly, hearing the capital letters in the name, even though the typical person on the street would have no idea what you're talking about.

Everyone loves their superlatives, too. The northernmost engagement. The bloodiest day. The bloodiest battle. The greatest victory. The most lopsided

defeat. All make great attention-grabbers.

That's why the Bloody Angle gets some attention. It was "the most savage hand-to-hand fighting." With a running time of 22 hours, the battle makes for an attention-grabber, indeed.

But Spotsylvania as a whole, and the Overland campaign in general, was all grit and no glory—"grim arithmetic," as I like to say. It was mud and maneuver and awful slaughter.

Spotsylvania offers a glimpse of the Overland campaign in miniature, the perfect illustration of the ongoing chess match between Grant and Lee as they poked and probed and marched and fought. The details of that strategic struggle largely get ignored—although that very strategy allowed Grant to eventually win the war. Rather, most people want "The Moment," the sensational story, the superlative. They don't want the grind.

George and Edward Stuart understood the power of that. The elder Stuart, George, president of the United States Christian Commission during the war, bought much

of the land around the Bloody Angle, and he and his son went to great lengths to preserve it for future generations. A monument to the younger Stuart once sat on the edge of a clearing opposite the angle, but the forest has grown up around it, and Edward Stuart and his monument have been forgotten. I remember trekking through the woods with a group of interns one year to show them. "Look at it," I told them. "The park does nothing to let people know it's here. No path. No wayside marker. No anything."

Is this the thanks a guy gets for doing so much to preserve the land? We wouldn't have this story to tell, wouldn't be able to tell it the way we do, if it wasn't for the Stuarts. Is this how we repay them? Do we even consider it a debt to repay? Hard to even remember a debt like that, I suppose, when most people hardly remember the battle itself.

Some of us are charged with remembering—like the Park Service, like historians and authors and scholars and guides. What responsibility do we have?

And what happens when even the stewards forget?

Stories go untold. Voices go unheard. Landscape goes uninterpreted.

My friend takes pictures. I write words. We try to see this land, share this story, so people won't forget.

SPOTSYLVANIA
COURT HOUSE

UNION ARMY Lieut. Gen. Ulysses S. Grant

ARMY OF THE POTOMAC Maj. Gen. George G. Meade
PROVOST GUARD Brig. Gen. Marsena R. Patrick
1st Massachusetts Cavalry, Companies C and D · 80th New York Infantry (20th Militia)
3rd Pennsylvania Cavalry · 68th Pennsylvania Infantry · 114th Pennsylvania Infantry

VOLUNTEER ENGINEER BRIGADE Brig. Gen. Henry W. Benham
15th New York Engineers · 50th New York Engineers · Battalion U.S. Engineers

GUARDS AND ORDERLIES *Independent Company Oneida (New York) Cavalry*

SECOND ARMY CORPS Maj. Gen. Winfield Scott Hancock
Escort *1st Vermont Cavalry, Company M*

First Division Brig. Gen. Francis C. Barlow
First Brigade Col. Nelson A. Miles
26th Michigan · 61st New York · 81st Pennsylvania · 140th Pennsylvania · 183rd Pennsylvania

Second Brigade Col. Thomas A. Smyth; Col. Richard Byrnes
28th Massachusetts · 63rd New York · 69th New York · 88th New York · 116th Pennsylvania

Third Brigade Col. Paul Frank; Col. Hiram R. Brown
39th New York · 52nd New York · 57th New York · 111th New York · 125th New York
126th New York

Fourth Brigade Col. John R. Brooke
2nd Delaware · 64th New York · 66th New York · 53rd Pennsylvania · 145th Pennsylvania
148th Pennsylvania

Second Division Brig. Gen. John Gibbon
Provost Guard *2nd Company Minnesota Sharpshooters*

First Brigade Brig. Gen. Alexander S. Webb; Col. H. Boyd McKeen
19th Maine · 1st Company Andrew (Massachusetts) Sharpshooters · 15th Massachusetts
19th Massachusetts · 20th Massachusetts · 7th Michigan · 42nd New York · 59th New York
82nd New York (2nd Militia)

160

Second Brigade Brig. Gen. Joshua T. Owen
152nd New York · 69th Pennsylvania · 71st Pennsylvania · 72nd Pennsylvania
106th Pennsylvania

Third Brigade Col. Samuel S. Carroll; Col. Thomas A. Smyth
14th Connecticut · 1st Delaware · 14th Indiana · 12th New Jersey · 10th New York Battalion
108th New York · 4th Ohio · 8th Ohio · 7th West Virginia

Fourth Brigade Col. Matthew Murphy; Col. James McIvor
155th New York · 164th New York · 170th New York · 182nd New York

Third Division Maj. Gen. David B. Birney
First Brigade Brig. Gen. J. H. Hobart Ward; Col. Thomas W. Egan
20th Indiana · 3rd Maine · 40th New York · 86th New York · 124th New York
99th Pennsylvania · 110th Pennsylvania · 141st Pennsylvania · 2nd U.S. Sharpshooters

Second Brigade Col. John S. Crocker; Col. Elijah Walker
4th Maine · 17th Maine · 3rd Michigan · 5th Michigan · 93rd New York
57th Pennsylvania · 63rd Pennsylvania · 105th Pennsylvania · 1st U.S. Sharpshooters

Fourth Division Brig. Gen. Gershom Mott[1]
First Brigade Col. Robert McAllister
1st Massachusetts · 16th Massachusetts · 5th New Jersey · 6th New Jersey · 7th New Jersey
8th New Jersey · 11th New Jersey · 26th Pennsylvania · 115th Pennsylvania

Second Brigade Col. William R. Brewster
11th Massachusetts · 70th New York · 71st New York · 72nd New York · 73rd New York
74th New York · 120th New York · 84th Pennsylvania

Fourth Division Brig. Gen. Robert O. Tyler[2]
1st Maine Heavy Artillery · 1st Massachusetts Heavy Artillery · 2nd New York Heavy Artillery
7th New York Heavy Artillery · 8th New York Heavy Artillery

Artillery Brigade Col. John C. Tidball
Maine Light, 6th Battery (F) · Massachusetts Light, 10th Battery · New Hamsphire Light, 1st Battery
1st New Jersey Light, Battery B[3] · 1st New York Light, Battery G · 4th New York Heavy, 3d Battalion
New York Light, 11th Battery[4] · New York Light, 12th Battery[5] · 1st Pennsylvania Light, Battery F
1st Rhode Island Light, Battery A · 1st Rhode Island Light, Battery B · 4th United States, Battery K
5th United States, Batteries C and I

FIFTH ARMY CORPS Maj. Gen. Gouverneur K. Warren
Provost Guard *12th New York Battalion*

First Division Brig. Gen. Charles Griffin
First Brigade Brig. Gen. Romeyn Ayres
140th New York · 146th New York · 91st Pennsylvania · 155th Pennsylvania
2nd United States, Companies B, C, F, H, I, and K
11th United States, Companies B, C, D, E, F, and G, First Battalion
12th United States, Companies A, B, C, D, and G, 1st Battalion

161

12th United States, Companies A, C, D, F, and H, 2d Battalion
14th United States, 1st Battalion
17th United States, Companies A, C, D, G, and H, 1st Battalion
17th United States, Companies A, B, and C, 2d Battalion

Second Brigade Col. Jacob Sweitzer
9th Massachusetts · 22nd Massachusetts · 32nd Massachusetts · 4th Michigan · 62nd Pennsylvania

Third Brigade Brig. Gen. Joseph J. Bartlett
20th Maine · 18th Massachusetts · 1st Michigan · 16th Michigan · 44th New York
83rd Pennsylvania · 118th Pennsylvania

Second Division[6] Brig. Gen. John C. Robinson
First Brigade[7] Col. Samuel Leonard
16th Maine · 13th Massachusetts · 39th Massachusetts · 104th New York · 90th Pennsylvania
107th Pennsylvania

Second Brigade[8] Brig. Gen. Henry Baxter; Col. Richard Coulter; Col. James L. Bates
12th Massachusetts · 83rd New York (9th Militia) · 97th New York · 11th Pennsylvania
88th Pennsylvania · 90th Pennsylvania

Third Brigade[9] Col. Andrew W. Denison; Col. Charles E. Phelps Jr.;
Col. Richard N. Bowerman
1st Maryland · 4th Maryland · 7th Maryland · 8th Maryland

Third Division Brig. Gen. Samuel W. Crawford
First Brigade Col. William McCandless; Col. Wellington N. Ent
1st Pennsylvania Reserves · 2nd Pennsylvania Reserves · 6th Pennsylvania Reserves
7th Pennsylvania Reserves · 11th Pennsylvania Reserves · 13th Pennsylvania Reserves (1st Rifles)

Third Brigade Col. Joseph W. Fisher
5th Pennsylvania Reserves · 8th Pennsylvania Reserves · 10th Pennsylvania Reserves
12th Pennsylvania Reserves

Fourth Division Brig. Gen. Lysander Cutler
First Brigade Brig. Gen. William W. Robinson
7th Indiana · 19th Indiana · 24th Michigan · 1st New York Battalion Sharpshooters
2nd Wisconsin · 6th Wisconsin · 7th Wisconsin

Second Brigade Brig. Gen. James C. Rice; Col. Edward B. Fowler;
Col. William J. Hoffman
76th New York · 84th New York (14th Militia) · 95th New York · 147th New York ·
56th Pennsylvania

Third Brigade Col. Edward S. Bragg
121st Pennsylvania · 142rd Pennsylvania · 143rd Pennsylvania · 149th Pennsylvania
150th Pennsylvania

Heavy Artillery Brigade
6th New York Heavy Artillery · 15th New York Heavy Artillery (2 Battalions)
4th New York Heavy Artillery (2nd Battalions)

ARTILLERY BRIGADE Col. Charles S. Wainwright
Massachusetts Light, Battery C · Massachusetts Light, Battery E · Massachusetts Light, 9th Battery[10]
1st New York Light, Battery B[11] · 1st New York Light, Battery C[12] · 1st New York Light, Battery D
1st New York Light, Batteries E and L · 1st New York Light, Battery H · New York Light, 5th Battery[13]
New York Light, 15th Battery[14] · 4th New York Heavy, 2nd Battalion
1st Pennsylvania Light, Battery B · 4th United States, Battery B · 5th United States, Battery D

SIXTH ARMY CORPS Maj. Gen. John Sedgwick; Brig. Gen. Horatio G. Wright
ESCORT *8th Pennsylvania Cavalry, Company A*

First Division Brig. Gen. Horatio G. Wright; Brig. Gen. David A. Russell
First Brigade Col. Henry W. Brown
1st New Jersey · 2nd New Jersey · 3rd New Jersey · 4th New Jersey · 10th New Jersey
15th New Jersey

Second Brigade Col. Emory Upton
5th Maine · 121st New York · 95th Pennsylvania · 96th Pennsylvania
2nd Connecticut Heavy Artillery[15]

Third Brigade Brig. Gen. David A. Russell; Col. Oliver Edwards
6th Maine · 49th Pennsylvania · 119th Pennsylvania · 5th Wisconsin

Fourth Brigade Brig. Gen. Alexander Shaler; Col. Nelson Cross
65th New York · 67th New York · 122nd New York · 82nd Pennsylvania

Second Division Brig. Gen. Thomas H. Neill
First Brigade Brig. Gen. Frank Wheaton
62nd New York · 93rd Pennsylvania · 98th Pennsylvania · 102nd Pennsylvania
139th Pennsylvania

Second Brigade Col. Lewis A. Grant
2nd Vermont · 3rd Vermont · 4th Vermont · 5th Vermont · 6th Vermont
1st Vermont Heavy Artillery[16]

Third Brigade Col. Daniel D. Bidwell
7th Maine · 43rd New York · 49th New York · 77th New York · 61st Pennsylvania

Fourth Brigade Brig. Gen. Henry L. Eustis
7th Massachusetts · 10th Massachusetts · 37th Massachusetts · 2nd Rhode Island

Third Division Brig. Gen. James B. Ricketts
First Brigade Brig. Gen. William H. Morris; Col. John W. Schall
14th New Jersey · 106th New York · 151st New York · 87th Pennsylvania · 10th Vermont

Second Brigade Col. Benjamin F. Smith
6th Maryland · 110th Ohio · 122nd Ohio · 126th Ohio · 67th Pennsylvania · 138th Pennsylvania

ARTILLERY BRIGADE Col. Charles H. Tompkins
Maine Light, 4th Battery (D) · Maine Light, Battery E[17] · Massachusetts Light, 1st Battery (A)
1st New Jersey Light, Battery A[18] · New York Light, 1st Battery · New York Light, 3rd Battery
4th New York Heavy, 1st Battalion · 1st Ohio Light, Battery H[19] · 1st Rhode Island Light. Battery C
1st Rhode Island Light, Battery E · 1st Rhode Island Light, Battery G · 5th United States, Battery E[20]
5th United States, Battery M

Unattached
NINTH ARMY CORPS Maj. Gen. Ambrose E. Burnside
PROVOST GUARD *8th U.S. Infantry*

First Division Brig. Gen. Thomas G. Stevenson; Col. Daniel Leasure;
Brig. Gen. Thomas Crittenden
First Brigade Lt. Col. Stephen M. Welsh Jr.; Brig. Gen. James H. Ledlie
35th Massachusetts · 56th Massachusetts · 57th Massachusetts · 59th Massachusetts
4th United States · 10th United States

Second Brigade Col. Daniel Leasure; Col. Joseph M. Sudsburg
3rd Maryland · 21st Massachusetts · 100th Pennsylvania

Artillery
Maine Light, 2nd Battery (B)
Massachusetts Light, 14th Battery

Second Division Brig. Gen. Robert B. Potter
First Brigade Col. Zenas R. Bliss; Col. John I. Curtain
36th Massachusetts · 58th Massachusetts · 51st New York · 45th Pennsylvania · 48th Pennsylvania
7th Rhode Island

Second Brigade Col. Simon G. Griffin
31st Maine · 32nd Maine · 6th New Hampshire · 9th New Hampshire · 11th New Hampshire
17th Vermont

Artillery
Massachusetts Light, 11th Battery · New York Light, 19th Battery

Third Division Brig. Gen. Orlando B. Willcox
First Brigade Col. John F. Hartranft
2nd Michigan · 8th Michigan · 17th Michigan · 27th Michigan · 109th New York
51st Pennsylvania

Second Brigade Col. Benjamin C. Christ; Col. William Humphrey
1st Michigan Sharpshooters · 20th Michigan · 70th New York · 60th Ohio · 50th Pennsylvania

Artillery
Maine Light, 7th Battery (G) · New York Light. 34th Battery

Fourth Division Brig Gen. Edward Ferrero
First Brigade Col. Joshua K. Sigfried
27th U. S. Colored Troops · 30th U.S. Colored Troops · 39th U.S. Colored Troops
43rd U.S. Colored Troops

Second Brigade Col. Henry G. Thomas
30th Connecticut (colored), detachment · 19th U.S. Colored Troops · 23rd U.S. Colored Troops

Artillery
Pennsylvania Light, Battery D · Vermont Light, 3d Battery

CAVALRY
3rd New Jersey · 22nd New York · 2nd Ohio · 13th Pennsylvania

RESERVE ARTILLERY Capt. John Edwards Jr.
New York Light. 27th Battery · 1st Rhode Island Light, Battery D · 1st Rhode Island Light, Battery H
2nd United States, Battery E · 3rd United States. Battery G · 3rd United States, Batteries L and M

PROVISIONAL BRIGADE Col. Elisha G. Marshall
24th New York Cavalry (dismounted) · 14th New York Heavy Artillery
2nd Pennsylvania Provisional Heavy Artillery

CAVALRY CORPS Maj. Gen. Philip H. Sheridan
Escort *6th United States*

First Division Brig. Gen. Wesley Merritt
First Brigade Brig. Gen. George A. Custer
1st Michigan · 5th Michigan · 6th Michigan · 7th Michigan

Second Brigade Col. Thomas C. Devin
4th New York · 6th New York · 9th New York · 17th Pennsylvania

Reserve Brigade Col. Alfred Gibbs
19th New York (1st Dragoons) · 6th Pennsylvania · 1st United States · 2nd United States
5th United States

Second Division Brig. Gen. David McM. Gregg
First Brigade Brig. Gen. Henry E. Davies Jr.
1st Massachusetts · 1st New Jersey · 6th Ohio · 1st Pennsylvania

Second Brigade Col. J. Irvin Gregg
1st Maine · 10th New York · 2nd Pennsylvania · 4th Pennsylvania · 8th Pennsylvania
16th Pennsylvania

Third Division Brig. Gen. James H. Wilson
Escort 8th Illinois (detachment)

First Brigade Col. John B. McIntosh
1st Connecticut · 2nd New York · 5th New York · 18th Pennsylvania

Second Brigade Col. George H. Chapman
3rd Indiana · 8th New York · 1st Vermont

ARTILLERY Brig. Gen. Henry J. Hunt
Artillery Reserve Col. Henry S. Burton
First Brigade Col. J. Howard Kitching
6th New York Heavy · 15th New York Heavy

Second Brigade Maj. John A. Tompkins
Maine Light, 5th Battery (E) · 1st New Jersey Light, Battery A · 1st New Jersey Light, Battery B
New York Light, 5th Battery · New York Light, 12th Battery · 1st New York Light, Battery B

Third Brigade Maj. Robert H. Fitzhugh
Massachusetts Light, 9th Battery · New York Light, 15th Battery · 1st New York Light, Battery C
New York Light, 11th Battery · 1st Ohio Light, Battery H · 5th United States, Battery E

Horse Artillery
First Brigade Capt. James M. Robertson
New York Light, 6th Battery · 2nd United States, Batteries B and L · 2nd United States, Battery D
2nd United States, Battery M 4th United States, Battery A · 4th United States, Batteries C and E

Second Brigade Capt. Dunbar R. Ransom
1st United States, Batteries E and G · 1st United States, Batteries H and I
1st United States, Battery K · 2nd United States, Battery A · 2nd United States, Battery G
3rd United States, Batteries C, F, and K

*   *   *

1 Division disbanded on May 13.
2 Division arrived on May 18.
3 Transferred from artillery Reserve on May 16.
4 Ibid.
5 Ibid.
6 Division disbanded on May 9.
7 Transferred to 4th Division.
8 Transferred to 2nd Division.
9 Transferred to 4th Division.
10 Transferred from Artillery Reserve May 16.
11 Ibid.
12 Ibid.
13 Ibid.
14 Ibid.
15 Attached May 21.
16 Attached May 14.
17 Transferred from Artillery Reserve May 16.
18 Ibid.
19 Ibid.
20 Ibid.

ARMY OF NORTHERN VIRGINIA Gen. Robert E. Lee

FIRST ARMY CORPS Maj. Gen. Richard H. Anderson
Kershaw's Division Brig. Gen. Joseph B. Kershaw
Kershaw's Brigade Col. John W. Henagan
2nd South Carolina · 3rd South Carolina · 7th South Carolina · 8th South Carolina
15th South Carolina · 3rd South Carolina Battalion

Wofford's Brigade Brig. Gen. William T. Wofford
16th Georgia · 18th Georgia · 24th Georgia · Cobb's (Georgia) Legion · Phillips (Georgia) Legion
3rd Georgia Battalion Sharpshooters

Humphreys' Brigade Brig. Gen. Benjamin Humphreys
13th Mississippi · 17th Mississippi · 18th Mississippi · 21st Mississippi

Bryan's Brigade Brig. Gen. Goode Bryan
10th Georgia · 50th Georgia · 51st Georgia · 53rd Georgia

Field's Division Maj. Gen. Charles W. Field
Jenkins' Brigade Col. John Bratton
1st South Carolina · 2nd South Carolina (Rifles) · 5th South Carolina · 6th South Carolina
Palmetto (South Carolina) Sharpshooters

Law's Brigade Col. William F. Perry; Brig. Gen Evander McIver Law
4th Alabama · 15th Alabama · 44th Alabama · 47th Alabama · 48th Alabama

Anderson's Brigade Brig. Gen. George T. Anderson
7th Georgia · 8th Georgia · 9th Georgia · 11th Georgia · 59th Georgia

Gregg's Brigade Brig. Gen. John Gregg
3rd Arkansas · 1st Texas · 4th Texas · 5th Texas

Benning's Brigade Col. Dudley M. Dubose
2nd Georgia · 15th Georgia · 17th Georgia · 20th Georgia

Artillery Brig. Gen. Edward Porter Alexander
Huger's Battalion Lieut. Col. Frank Huger
Fickling's (South Carolina) battery · Moody's (Louisiana) battery · Parker's (Virginia) battery
Smith's, J. D. (Virginia), battery · Taylor's (Virginia) battery · Woolfolk's (Virginia) battery

Haskell's Battalion Maj. John C. Haskell
Flanner's (North Carolina) battery · Garden's (South Carolina) battery
Lamkin's (Virginia) battery (unequipped) · Ramsay's (North Carolina) battery

Cabell's Battalion Col. Henry C. Cabell
Callaway's (Georgia) battery · Carlton's (Georgia) battery · McCarthy's (Virginia.) battery
Manly's (North Carolina) battery

167

SECOND ARMY CORPS Lieut. Gen. Richard S. Ewell
Early's Division Maj. Gen. Jubal A. Early; Brig. Gen. John B. Gordon
Pegram's Brigade Brig. Gen. John Pergram
13th Virginia · 31st Virginia · 49th Virginia · 52nd Virginia · 58th Virginia

Gordon's Brigade Col. Clement Evans
13th Georgia · 26th Georgia · 31st Georgia · 38th Georgia · 60th Georgia · 61st Georgia

Johnston's Brigade Brig. Gen. Robert D. Johnston; Col. Thomas F. Toon
5th North Carolina · 12th North Carolina · 20th North Carolina · 23rd North Carolina

Johnson's Division[1] Maj. Gen. Edward "Alleghany" Johnson
Stonewall Brigade[2] Brig. Gen. James A. Walker
2nd Virginia · 4th Virginia · 5th Virginia · 27th Virginia · 33rd Virginia

Jones' Brigade[3] Brig. Gen. John M. Jones
21st Virginia · 25th Virginia · 42nd Virginia · 44th Virginia · 48th Virginia · 50th Virginia

Steuart's Brigade[4] Brig. Gen. George H. "Maryland" Steuart
1st North Carolina · 3rd North Carolina · 10th Virginia · 23rd Virginia · 37th Virginia

Stafford's Brigade Brig. Gen. Harry Hays; Col. Zebulon York
5th Louisiana · 6th Louisiana · 7th Louisiana · 8th Louisiana · 9th Louisiana · 1st Louisiana
2nd Louisiana · 10th Louisiana · 14th Louisiana · 15th Louisiana

Rodes' Division Maj. Gen. Robert E. Rodes
Daniel's Brigade Brig. Gen. Junius Daniel
32nd North Carolina · 43rd North Carolina · 45th North Carolina · 53d North Carolina
2nd North Carolina Battalion

Doles' Brigade Brig. Gen. George Doles
4th Georgia · 12th Georgia · 44th Georgia

Ramseur's Brigade Brig. Gen. Stephen D. Ramseur
2nd North Carolina · 4th North Carolina · 14th North Carolina · 30th North Carolina

Battle's Brigade Brig. Gen. Cullen A. Battle
3rd Alabama · 5th Alabama · 6th Alabama · 12th Alabama · 26th Alabama

Johnston's Brigade Brig. Gen. Robert D. Johnston
5th North Carolina · 12th North Carolina · 20th North Carolina · 23rd North Carolina

Artillery Brig. Gen. Armistead L. Long
Hardaway's Battalion Lieut. Col. Robert A. Hardaway
Dance's (Virginia) battery · Graham's (Virginia) battery · Griffin's, C. B. (Virginia), battery
Jones' (Virginia) battery · Smith's, B. H. (Virginia), battery

Braxton's Battalion Lieut. Col. Carter M. Braxton
Carpenter's (Virginia) battery · Cooper's (Virginia) battery · Hardwicke's (Virginia) battery

Nelson's Battalion Lieut. Col. William Nelson
Kirkpatrick's (Virginia) battery · Massie's (Virginia) battery · Milledge's (Georgia) battery

Cutshaw's Battalion Maj. Wilfred E. Cutshaw
Carrington's (Virginia) battery · Garber's, A. W. (Virginia), battery · Tanner's (Virginia) battery

Page's Battalion Maj. Richard C. M. Page
Carter's, W. P. (Virginia), battery · Fry's (Virginia) battery · Page's (Virginia) battery
Reese's (Alabama) battery

THIRD ARMY CORPS Lt. Gen. A. P. Hill; Maj. Gen. Jubal A. Early
Anderson's Division Brig. Gen. William Mahone
Perrin's Brigade Brig. Gen. Abner Perrin; Col. John C. C. Sanders
8th Alabama · 9th Alabama · 10th Alabama · 11th Alabama · 14th Alabama

Harris' Brigade Brig. Gen. Nathaniel H. Harris
12th Mississippi · 16th Mississippi · 19th Mississippi · 48th Mississippi

Mahone's Brigade Col. David A. Weiseger
6th Virginia · 12th Virginia · 16th Virginia · 41st Virginia · 61st Virginia

Wright's Brigade Brig. Gen. Amrose R. Wright
3rd Georgia · 22nd Georgia · 48th Georgia · 2nd Georgia Battalion

Perry's Brigade Brig. Gen. Edward A. Perry
2nd Florida · 5th Florida · 8th Florida

Heth's Division Maj. Gen. Henry Heth
Davis' Brigade Brig. Gen. Joseph R. Davis
2nd Mississippi · 11th Mississippi · 42nd Mississippi · 55th North Carolina

Cooke's Brigade Brig. Gen. John R. Cooke
15th North Carolina · 27th North Carolina · 46th North Carolina · 48th North Carolina

Kirkland's Brigade Brig. Gen. William W. Kirkland
11th North Carolina · 26th North Carolina · 44th North Carolina · 47th North Carolina
52nd North Carolina

Walker's Brigade Brig. Gen. Henry H. Walker; Col. Robert M. Mayo
40th Virginia · 47th Virginia · 55th Virginia · 22nd Virginia Battalion · 13th Alabama
1st Tennessee (Provisional Army) · 7th Tennessee · 14th Tennessee

Wilcox's Division Maj. Gen. Cadmus M. Wilcox
Lane's Brigade Brig. Gen. James H. Lane
7th North Carolina · 18th North Carolina · 28th North Carolina · 33rd North Carolina
37th North Carolina

169

Scales' Brigade Brig. Gen. Alfred M. Scales
13th North Carolina · 16th North Carolina · 22nd North Carolina · 34th North Carolina
38th North Carolina

McGowan's Brigade Brig. Gen. Samuel McGowan; Col. Joseph N. Brown
1st South Carolina (Provisional Army) · 12th South Carolina · 13th South Carolina
14th South Carolina · 1st South Carolina (Orr's Rifles)

Thomas' Brigade Brig. Gen. Edward R. Thomas
14th Georgia · 35th Georgia · 45th Georgia · 49th Georgia

Artillery Col. R. Lindsay Walker
Poague's Battalion Lieut. Col. William T. Poague
Richards' (Mississippi) battery · Utterback's (Virginia) battery · Williams' (North Carolina) battery
Wyatt's (Virginia) battery

Pegram's Battalion Lieut. Col. William J. Pegram
Brander's (Virginia) battery · Cayce's (Virginia) battery · Ellett's (Virginia) battery
Marye's (Virginia) battery · Zimmerman's (South Carolina) battery

McIntosh' s Battalion Lieut. Col. David G. McIntosh
Clutter's (Virginia) battery · Donald's (Virginia) battery · Hurt's (Alabama) battery
Price's (Virginia) battery

Cutts' Battalion Col. Allen S. Cutts
Patterson's (Georgia) battery · Ross' (Georgia) battery · Wingfield's (Georgia) battery

Richardson's Battalion Lieut. Col. Charles Richardson
Grandy's (Virginia) battery · Landry's (Louisiana) battery · Moore's (Virginia) battery
Penick's (Virginia) battery

CAVALRY CORPS Maj. Gen. James E. B. Stuart
Hampton's Division Maj. Gen. Wade Hampton
Young's Brigade Brig. Gen. Pierce M. B. Young
7th Georgia · Cobb's (Georgia) Legion · Phillips (Georgia) Legion · 20th Georgia Battalion
Jeff. Davis (Mississippi) Legion

Rosser's Brigade Brig. Gen. Thomas L. Rosser
7th Virginia · 11th Virginia · 12th Virginia · 35th Virginia Battalion

Butler's Brigade Brig. Gen. Matthew C. Butler
4th South Carolina · 5th South Carolina · 6th South Carolina

Fitzhugh Lee's Division Maj. Gen. Fitzhugh Lee
Lomax's Brigade Brig. Gen. Lunsford L. Lomax
5th Virginia · 6th Virginia · 15th Virginia

Wickham's Brigade Brig. Gen. Williams C. Wickham
1st Virginia · 2nd Virginia · 3rd Virginia · 4th Virginia

William H. F. Lee's Division Maj. Gen. William H. F. Lee
Chambliss' Brigade Brig. Gen. John R. Chambliss, Jr.
9th Virginia · 10th Virginia · 13th Virginia
Gordon's Brigade Brig. Gen. James B. Gordon; Col. Clinton M. Andrews
1st North Carolina · 2nd North Carolina · 5th North Carolina

Horse Artillery Maj. R. Preston Chew
Breathed's Battalion Maj. James Breathed
Hart's (South Carolina) battery · Johnston's (Virginia) battery
McGregor's (Virginia) battery · Shoemaker's (Virginia) battery
Thomson's (Virginia) battery

1 Division ceased to exist on May 13, units were formally parceled out to other brigades and divisions on May 21.
2 Formally consolidated into Brig. William Terry's brigade on May 21.
3 Formally consolidated into Brig. William Terry's brigade on May 21.
4 Formally consolidated into Brig. William Terry's and Brig. Gen. Stephen D. Ramseur's brigades
on May 21.

Suggested Reading

SPOTSYLVANIA COURT HOUSE

And Keep Moving On: The Virginia Campaign May-June 1864
Mark Grimsley
University of Nebraska Press (2002)
ISBN-13: 978-0803271197 (paperback, 2005)

A book that proves the adage "Don't judge a book by its cover." The cover features a painting of VMI's Cadet Corps charging at New Market—which *did* happen in Virginia May of 1864—but Grimsley's book is actually a highly readable one-volume account of the Overland campaign.

If It Takes All Summer: The Battle of Spotsylvania
William D. Matter
University of North Carolina Press (1988)
ISBN-13: 978-0807817810 (hardcover)

Matter provided the first book-length study on Spotsylvania, setting a high bar for the works that followed. The text is dense but the research thorough and the narrative clear.

*The Battles for Spotsylvania Court House
and the Road to Yellow Tavern*
Gordon C. Rhea
Louisiana State University Press (1994)
ISBN-13: 978-0807130674 (paperback, 2005)

To the North Anna River: Grant and Lee, May 13-25, 1864
Gordon C. Rhea
Louisiana State University Press (2000)
ISBN-13: 978-0807131114 (paperback, 2005)

Gordon Rhea sets the standard for all battlefield studies
with his marvelous four-volume series on the Overland
Campaign. The two middle volumes focus on the action
at Spotsylvania Court House, including a thorough
account of Jeb Stuart's last battle at Yellow Tavern and
taking the narrative all the way through the action at
North Anna. The series is bookended by volumes on
the Wilderness and Cold Harbor. His abundant use of
primary source material and his engaging narrative make
his work must-read.

*Bloody Roads South: The Wilderness to Cold Harbor, May-June
1864*
Noah Andre Trudeau
Louisiana State University Press (1989)
ISBN-13: 978-0807126448 (paperback, 2000)

A "popular history" of the Overland campaign, Trudeau's
work focuses on story over research, making it accessible
to wide audiences.

About the Authors

Chris Mackowski, Ph.D., is a professor in the School of Journalism and Mass Communication at St. Bonaventure University in Allegany, NY. He also works as a historian with the National Park Service at Fredericksburg and Spotsylvania National Military Park, where he gives tours at four major Civil War battlefields (Fredericksburg, Chancellorsville, Wilderness, and Spotsylvania), as well as at the building where Stonewall Jackson died. He's the author of *Chancellorsville: Crossroads of Fire* and *The Dark, Close Wood: The Wilderness, Ellwood, and the Battle that Transformed Both,* and his writing has appeared in several national magazines. He blogs regularly for *Scholars and Rogues* (www.scholarsandrogues.com).

Kristopher D. White is a historian for the Penn-Trafford Recreation Board and a continuing education instructor for the Community College of Allegheny County near Pittsburgh, PA. White is a graduate of Norwich University with a M.A. in Military History, as well as a graduate of California University of Pennsylvania with a B.A. in History. For five years he served as a staff military historian at Fredericksburg and Spotsylvania National Military Park, where he still volunteers his services. For a short time, he was a member of the Association of Licensed Battlefield Guides at Gettysburg. Over the past seven years, he has spoken to more than thirty roundtables and historical societies.

Chris and **Kris**, longtime friends, have co-authored several books together, including *The Last Days of Stonewall Jackson, Chancellorsville's Forgotten Front: The Battles of Second Fredericksburg and Salem Church,* and *Simply Murder: The Battle of Fredericksburg,* along with monograph-length articles on the battle of Spotsylvania for *Blue & Gray*. Mackowski and White have also written for *Civil War Times, America's Civil War,* and *Hallowed Ground*. They are co-founders of the blog *Emerging Civil War* (www.emergingcivilwar.com).

EMERGING CIVIL WAR SERIES